TAKING CENTER

a lifetime of live performance
NEIL PEART

by Joe Bergamini

HUDSON MUSIC®

CONTENTS

Foreword_____5

Introduction_____6

About This Book_____8

The Making of *Taking Center Stage*_____14

Drum Key_____30

CHAPTER 1: 2112 and All the World's a Stage Tours (1976-77)_____33
Drum Setup 35

CHAPTER 2: A Farewell to Kings Tour (1977)_____36
Drum Setup 39

CHAPTER 3: Hemispheres Tour (1978-79)_____40
Drum Setup 42
"The Trees" 43 ■ Analysis 43 ■ Drum Transcription 45
"La Villa Strangiato" 49 ■ Analysis 49 ■ Drum Transcription 51

CHAPTER 4: Permanent Waves Tour (1979-80)_____58
Drum Setup 60
"The Spirit of Radio" 61 ■ Analysis 61 ■ Drum Transcription 62
"Free Will" 66 ■ Analysis 66 ■ Drum Transcription 68
"Natural Science" 73 ■ Analysis 73 ■ Drum Transcription 75

CHAPTER 5: Moving Pictures Tour (1980-81)_____81
Drum Setup 84
"Tom Sawyer" 85 ■ Analysis 85 ■ Drum Transcription 87
"YYZ" 91 ■ Analysis 91 ■ Drum Transcription 93

CHAPTER 6: Signals Tour (1982-83)_____97
Drum Setup 101
"Subdivisions" 102 ■ Analysis 102 ■ Drum Transcription 104

CHAPTER 7: Grace Under Pressure and
Power Windows Tours (1984-86)_____108
Drum Setup 113
"Marathon" 114 ■ Analysis 115 ■ Drum Transcription 116

CHAPTER 8:   Hold Your Fire Tour (1987-88)_____122

Drum Setup 126
"Time Stand Still" 128 ■ Analysis 128 ■ Drum Transcription 129

CHAPTER 9:   Presto Tour (1990)_____134

Drum Setup 136
"Presto" 138 ■ Analysis 138 ■ Drum Transcription 140

CHAPTER 10:   Roll the Bones and
Counterparts Tours (1991-92, 1994)_____144

Drum Setup 147
"Bravado" 149 ■ Analysis 149 ■ Drum Transcription 150
"Leave That Thing Alone!" 153 ■ Analysis 153 ■ Drum Transcription 155

CHAPTER 11:   Test for Echo Tour (1996-97)_____159

Drum Setup 162

CHAPTER 12:   Vapor Trails Tour (2002)_____164

Drum Setup 168

CHAPTER 13:   R30 Tour (2004)_____169

Drum Setup 174

CHAPTER 14:   Snakes & Arrows Tour (2007-08)_____175

Drum Setup 178
"Workin' Them Angels" 179 ■ Analysis 179 ■ Drum Transcription 180
"Far Cry" 184 ■ Analysis 184 ■ Drum Transcription 186

CHAPTER 15:   Time Machine Tour (2011)_____190

Drum Setup 192
"BU2B " 193 ■ Analysis 193 ■ Drum Transcription 194
"Caravan" 198 ■ Analysis 198 ■ Drum Transcription 199

Source List_____204
About the Author_____206

CREDITS

By Joe Bergamini
Additional Editing by Neil Peart
Music Transcriptions by Joe Bergamini
Book Design and Layout by Rick Gratton
Music Engraving and Additional Music Editing by Willie Rose
Cover Design by Hugh Syme
Original Rush album art and design elements by Hugh Syme
Text Edited by Jill Flomenhoft
Executive Producers: Rob Wallis and Paul Siegel

Photography Credits:

Front Cover Photo by Andrew MacNaughtan

Back Cover Photo by Fin Costello

Andrew MacNaughtan: pages 121, 134, 137 bottom, 144, 146, 148, 149, 159, 163, 166, 170, 173 bottom left and right, 185, 189 top, 190, 203 top

Rick Gould: pages 81, 83, 100, 108, 112 center, 114, 122, 137 top, 161, 164, 167 bottom, 169, 173 top, 175, 177, 179, 183, 203 bottom

Clayton Call: pages 6, 7, 8, 9, 11, 12-13, 16, 17, 18, 19, 20, 22, 30-31, 206

Fin Costello: pages 33, 35, 36, 38, 40, 58, 67 © Fin Costello/fincostello.com

Gene Ambo: pages 110, 124, 125, 127

Courtesy of Tama Drums: pages 60, 97, 98, 115

Courtesy of Zildjian Cymbals: page 98 top and bottom

Rob Wallis: pages 10, 21, 23, 25, 29 top left, middle left, and bottom

Paul Siegel: pages 15, 24 bottom, 28

Joe Bergamini: pages 29 middle right, 189 center and bottom, 207 bottom left

Neil Peart: page 24 top

Fred Carneau: page 32

Greg Ouzunoff: page 34

Gregory McKean: page 172

Mark Gelvan: page 207 bottom right

All photos are the property of their respective photographers and are used by permission.

Modern Drummer® magazine covers and advertisements courtesy of Modern Drummer® Publications.

Very special thanks to Pegi Cecconi at SRO/Anthem for her assistance with this project.

Special thanks for assistance with photo research and procurement to Adam Budofsky and Scott Bienstock at Modern Drummer Publications, Jim Gallagher and Happy Yoshida at Tama Drums/Hoshino Gakki Co., Jim Catalano at Ludwig Drums, and Scott Donnell at DW.

The author would like to thank the following people whose assistance helped make this project possible:

Neil Peart; Rob Wallis, Paul Siegel, and Alfonse Giordano at Hudson Music; Rick Gratton; Willie Rose; Pegi Cecconi, Meghan Symsyk, and Bob Farmer at SRO/Anthem Entertainment; Aaron Stang at Alfred Music Publishing Company; Hugh Syme; Adam Budofsky, Scott Bienstock, Michael Dawson, and all at Modern Drummer Publications; Rick Gould; Fin Costello; Dave Cywinski; Kimberly, Nicholas, and Jennarose Bergamini.

FOREWORD

By Neil Peart

Now seems a particularly fitting time for me to offer these words, as I am presently back working at Drum Channel, rehearsing for the *Clockwork Angels* tour—the "sequel" to Time Machine. Thus July 2012 finds me relaunching the entire process of planning, practice, and performance reflected in the *Taking Center Stage* DVD, and now in this book.

Every day I play along with a proposed set list of old and new songs, building stamina and calluses, and feeling my strength, accuracy, and confidence grow. Recently a notion occurred to me that very much ties together the musical odyssey that is documented by the songs and stories in the DVD and book:

The way I play now is the way I always *wanted* to play.

Meaning that right from the beginning, forty-seven years ago, my fairly obsessive dedication to the drums has been aiming at a nexus of technique and feel that I am only now starting to attain. After all that time, and having worked with my bandmates Alex and Geddy for almost thirty-eight years, I don't think it is immodest to say, "We have come a long way."

Living up to the true meaning of the oft-maligned word "progressive," we have consciously tried to get better—on our instruments, and in our songwriting, arranging, and performing. However, we have learned that such a path is never *linear*.

Technique can provide you with the tools to express a wider range of ideas and emotions—a component of music-making that can never be overemphasized. Yet, in a seeming contradiction, for the past fifteen years I have studied, practiced, and labored to make my playing looser and more improvisational—thus applying discipline to the pursuit of freedom.

(Reminds me of a lyric I took from some L.A. graffiti in the '70s: "You don't get freedom for free.")

So now, at the leading edge of that long train of years, teachers, practice, recordings, and concerts, I play the drums with what I can physically *feel* is a more refined combination of technique and natural motion—perhaps more pithily described as "chops and groove." That's the way I always wanted to play. Maybe it's too bad it took me forty-seven years to approach that desire—but, as my dear friend and teacher, the late Freddie Gruber, would have said, "It is what it is."

That long, *slow* train of my progress is well documented in this book—a historical retrospective of sorts, though the transcribed drum parts reflect the way I play *now*. It also blends three of my favorite "art languages"—words, musical notes, and images.

The historical pageant of photographs thoroughly documents the "gearhead" side of the journey, in the parade of drumsets (the "*hit* parade," heh-heh). Those images reflect another important side of my lifelong quest: the continuous refinement of "the voices."

Joe Bergamini (Jobee, to me) has done a wonderful—even heroic—job in assembling all of this material, and has given much of himself to the project. Even apart from the factual detail, Joe's insights and playing advice are worthwhile additions in their own right.

During the filming of the *Taking Center Stage* DVD, Joe and I worked closely with my previous instructional DVD collaborators, Paul Siegel and Rob Wallis, making it a four-way partnership.

However, this book is pretty much "all Joe," and the only thing that remains for me to say is, "Way to go, Joe!"

INTRODUCTION

In 2011, Hudson Music released *Taking Center Stage: A Lifetime of Live Performance*, our second DVD with Neil Peart. This DVD was unprecedented in scope, with Neil discussing and explaining his approach to many classic Rush songs. From the beginning, I intended to create a transcription book to accompany the DVD. Having worked on transcription books in the past, notably with Scott Rockenfield (Queensrÿche), Chris Pennie (Dillinger Escape Plan), and Jason Bittner (Shadows Fall), I developed what I felt was a more interesting approach to the typical transcription book. In addition to musical notation, I included drumset diagrams, album artwork, photos, and interviews with the artists. It had been my hope that these books would therefore be accessible to a wider audience, namely drummers who do not read music, and even general fans, who might glean some information about their favorite band that was not available elsewhere.

Like many other drummers my age, Neil was my first drum hero. I spent hour upon hour practicing to Rush music in my parents' basement. Working on the DVD with him was a dream come true, but I also wanted to present something more: the definitive book about Neil that I always wished I had when I was a kid. That is what I've tried to create here. This book contains so much more than just music transcriptions; it's a retrospective documentation on one of the most creative drummers in modern music history. The reason Neil has captured the imagination of so many people is the creativity and artistic vision with which he approaches every aspect of his work. It is this artistic vision that I have tried to reflect with this book: All of the explanatory text analysis, the beautiful color photos, the album package artwork, the detailed drum transcriptions, the painstakingly researched drumset diagrams, and even the old magazine advertisements have come together to create something for the fan of Rush and Neil Peart to admire, learn from, and simply enjoy.

Perhaps for you, like me, some of these descriptions, photos, and graphics will bring back fond memories. So many famous drummers have talked about seeing Ringo Starr on "The Ed Sullivan Show" as the moment that set them on their life's path with drumming. Well for me, it was hearing Neil Peart on the radio with Rush, and seeing him at Madison Square Garden in 1984. I suspect that many of you reading this have similar stories.

I would like to thank Neil for not only overseeing this project, but for simply indulging my love of his band and his drumming in allowing me to put this book together. I hope you enjoy reading and looking at it as much as I enjoyed writing it.

About This Book

This book examines Neil Peart's approach to live performance by looking at the different Rush tours over the years, Neil's choice of equipment on each tour, and his current approach to performing certain songs live. The book is arranged in chronological order, with a chapter devoted to each tour. Each chapter contains the following:

1. An overview of the tour and the equipment Neil was using at the time.
2. A detailed diagram of the drum setup from that tour.
3. Excerpts from the Rush tour books, where Neil discusses his gear in his own words.
4. A text discussion of the songs included in that chapter (if any).
5. Text analysis of the drum parts for these songs.
6. Transcriptions of the songs from performances on the Time Machine tour (2011).
7. Photographs showing Neil and the drumset used on that tour.

About the Transcriptions:

It is important to note that all of the transcriptions contained in this book are taken from Neil's live performance on the Hudson Music DVD *Taking Center Stage: A Lifetime of Live Performance*, which is the companion to this book. In order to analyze the transcriptions and read along, you must also own the DVD. Although it is interesting (and recommended) to compare these transcriptions with Neil's performance on the original versions of these songs, it is important to understand that these transcriptions come from Neil's 2011 performances. The songs are arranged in chronological order, to match the album on which they originally appeared, so that as each tour and drumset are discussed, you can also check out one (or more) of the songs from that particular era. But remember, the transcriptions do not come from the original albums.

Transcribing a drum part is often a subjective process. Neil, like many of the greats, has a feel and sound that is impossible to notate on paper. It is highly recommended to spend time sitting with these transcriptions while listening along to the DVD. Only then will you have a chance to understand how Neil's touch and feel make him a unique player. These human elements are the things that make us all sound different from one another, and give each of us our individual style.

Having said that, I have done my best to notate every detail of what Neil has played in these songs. Being able to transcribe from a video is beneficial in this regard, because it allows the transcriber to see very soft ghost notes being played (whereas on a recording, these notes would not be heard, and so would not be written out). By watching Neil's hands and feet, I was able to include just about every note that he played. This includes ghost notes on the bass drum, which can be a tricky topic. When Neil plays the bass drum, there are incidental notes created by his foot technique. He plays with his heel up, and in the course of playing the groove, the beater often makes a soft impact with the head in the process of the muscles moving to create another note. Although this is a very common occurrence with drummers, in the context of a full mix of a concert or an album, the soft notes would not be heard. In the case of our DVD, the drums are presented so forward in the mix that all of this detail is audible. Therefore, I have chosen to include almost all of these bass-drum ghost notes. It is very important to listen to the DVD so that you can understand the interpretation of these notes. If your technique does not allow relaxed execution of the soft notes naturally, then you should omit them if you play along with the charts.

About the Drumset Diagrams:

Neil has captured the imagination of so many drummers because of his creativity and attention to detail concerning every aspect of his art, and this most definitely includes the design of his drumsets. All drummers love looking at each other's sets; they seem to be extensions of our personalities and artistic visions. Neil has always been one of the most interesting and creative artists in this respect; the design of his drumset is more than just the placement of the instruments. Thought has been given to everything from the design of the hardware, to the finish of the shells and hardware, and even to the design of the drum riser itself. Therefore, it was extremely important for me to depict each drumset in exacting detail. This took quite a bit of research.

I began with the tour books and a handful of books about Rush, including Robert Telleria's excellent book, *Rush: Merely Players*, which includes a detailed list of the equipment used by Neil over the years. Then, I enlisted the assistance of my friends at *Modern Drummer* in supplying back issues and digital copies of every piece about Neil they have ever done. Once I had a basic idea of the gear that was probably used on a given tour, I did extensive research using photographs from all the various tour books and all over the Internet to visually locate each piece of equipment on every drumset, for every tour. I wanted, for instance, to make sure I knew the exact number of Simmons pads that appeared on the white *Hold Your Fire* kit. I think I've been able to accurately document the equipment placement. If you compare the diagrams with the photographs, I think you will see everything represented properly.

Neil was also helpful with certain details. For instance, in the chapter about the *Permanent Waves* tour, he pointed out that the finish on his drumset was rosewood, modeled after some antique Chinese furniture he had at home (correcting my original description of the finish as "mahogany"). So of course, having Neil look everything over was a great advantage, and I am thankful to him for doing so.

As I envisioned this project, I was thoroughly excited about being able to take it far beyond a typical transcription book, and make it a much more engaging visual document about Neil. My criteria for including photographs was that each shot must show a considerable amount of the equipment that was used on each tour. I have always been enthralled with Neil's choice of gear, and I think most fans would agree that his drumset expresses his creativity so well, and is so interesting to look at. Therefore, I passed over some of the more typical "magazine-style" shots that might have an interesting facial expression, and instead chose a series of photographs that document Neil and his equipment over the years.

From the very beginning, I wanted to use a large number of photos from Rush's longtime official photographer, Andrew MacNaughtan. Unfortunately, Andrew passed away unexpectedly just as I began research for this book. We at Hudson Music are very grateful to his estate in allowing the use of his work, and to Pegi Cecconi at SRO/Anthem for facilitating the use of his photographs. No book about Neil could be published without photos from Andrew, and I am very pleased that we have been able to include a large selection of his shots.

A lot of other research went into finding photographs, and all of this began with a visit to the offices of *Modern Drummer* magazine, where my friends are always willing to assist me with any crazy project! In this case Editorial Director Adam Budofsky and Senior Art Director Scott Bienstock provided a large selection of Neil shots from over the years, and put me in touch with the various photographers. Among them was Rick Gould, who was extremely helpful in providing many shots that I needed, as well as being an absolute pleasure to work with.

The biggest challenge was getting some of the older shots of Neil, before Andrew became the official photographer. As a big Rush fan, of course I knew that Fin Costello was their official photographer in the early days. Happily, a quick online search led me to Fin, who turned out to be accommodating, interesting, and terrific to work with. I am thrilled that we were able to include some classic shots from Fin, especially those that document the kit from *A Farewell to Kings* in such wonderful detail.

Among the others who have contributed photos or assistance are the good people at Tama, Ludwig, Sabian, and Zildjian, and we thank them. Please see the credits for a detailed list of photographers.

13

THE MAKING OF TAKING CENTER STAGE
Working with Neil Peart

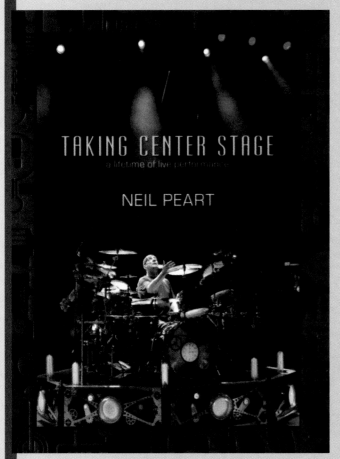

Waking just after sunrise, I stepped outside the door of my motel room in Stovepipe Wells, in Death Valley National Park, California. I had always wanted to see remote and breathtaking desert landscapes like this, but never really expected to have the opportunity. I took a short walk along the road next to the parking lot, admiring the sand dunes in the distance, and the jagged peaks of the Panamint Mountains marching away to the south. The tan of the desert sand mixing into the purple of the mountains and the deep blue of the early morning sky created one of those sights that you just take in for a moment, happy to be alive. I walked across the motel compound, past the stand of mesquite trees where a family of very large crows had kept watch over us for the last few days.

As I walked up the steps to the restaurant, I glanced over toward the parking lot, and it looked empty. I assumed the Ghost Rider had gone, and was speeding over some distant highway back toward the Pacific Ocean. I had planned on meeting the rest of the Hudson crew at 7 a.m. for breakfast, but was up early, so I figured I would get a cup of coffee, read, and enjoy the scenery. As the hostess led me toward the back of the restaurant, I rounded a corner and found that I had been mistaken—there was Neil Peart, the man who inspired an entire generation of guys like me to play drums, and one of the most revered rock musicians of all time, sitting there alone, looking over his journal. Even after having met him in 2008, and having worked fairly closely with him since then on the project which is the topic of this story, I paused. Neil glanced up, smiled, and invited me to join him. He showed me some of the newest "passport stamps" he had collected on his visits to national parks.

As we sat and talked for a few minutes, I couldn't help but smile to myself, and feel thankful for the opportunity to know and work with Neil over the last couple of years. He turned out to be everything I expected: hard-working, intelligent, interesting, focused, and creative—and, even better, a really nice guy as well. Soon we were joined by the rest of the Hudson guys, and enjoyed a hearty breakfast together before Neil set off for home.

This journey of working with Neil on his new Hudson Music DVD, *Taking Center Stage: A Lifetime of Live Performance*, has been one of the most amazing experiences of my life. In my position with Hudson Music, and in my travels as a professional drummer, I have been very fortunate to meet (and in some cases get to know) almost all of my favorite drummers. And, of course, working with Rob Wallis and Paul Siegel as their Senior Drum Editor for Hudson Music has been an honor in itself, since they have trusted me to collaborate with them on projects with some of the greatest drummers on the planet. I have been a huge Rush fan since I was 12 years old, and in my younger years Neil was my hero. I wore out my VHS copy of *Exit…Stage Left* by repeatedly playing the video in slow motion to try to see what Neil was doing. I have seen Rush in concert just about every time they have come to the New York area, and even spent ten years playing in a Rush tribute band.

But as a fan of Neil's, of course I became aware of his private lifestyle—exemplified by his never attending the kind of drum/music industry events at which I have met all the rest of my favorite drummers. Thus I believed I would never have the opportunity to meet him.

In early 2008, Paul and Rob mentioned to me that in conversations with Neil, they thought he might be open to the idea of doing another project. Having worked with Neil on both of his previous drum DVDs, they knew that he would not want to cover any of the same ground again, but would want to explore and explain new areas. Knowing how familiar I was with Neil's work, Paul and Rob asked me to create an outline and proposal for him. This was exciting, but a huge assignment: trying to come up with something that would be interesting enough for Neil to want to do. It was also a major project for Hudson, so I didn't want to screw it up!

I wanted to be able to discuss Neil's entire body of work, including all the classic songs that made him the most emulated rock drummer of the late 1970s and 1980s. However, I knew that Neil was a very forward-thinking artist, constantly in search of new ground, and not so interested in analyzing his past work. So this presented a structural challenge.

After bouncing several preliminary ideas off of Paul and Rob, the three of us took one of my extensive outlines covering Neil's entire body of work, and fine-tuned it into a presentation for him. They sent it to Neil for his opinion, as I waited anxiously. Finally word came back from Neil, and he seemed impressed by the concept that was presented, and even somewhat interested. Since he wanted to continue the conversation further, the guys suggested that they bring me to meet Neil, both so that he could get to know me a little, and potentially discuss the project further. I was pleased at this, but still a little unsure as to whether it would lead to actually working on a project with him.

On July 12, 2008, Rob Wallis and I met up in the early afternoon outside the PNC Bank Arts Center in Holmdel, New Jersey. I had seen Rush in concert there several times, and had always dreamed of going backstage to meet Neil. Now that day had arrived, but it was not for some autograph session. I was nervous. When it came right down to it, I started to feel that it would be much easier to just remain an admirer from afar, given what I thought Neil's reaction would be when he met someone like me, who was such a fan of his work. Finally the appointed time came, and we were ushered into (of all places) Neil's bus. Rob went in first, and I nervously ascended the steps and stood just inside the door. To Neil, of course, it was just another day at work, and he emerged from the back of the bus wearing a baseball hat, and gave Rob a hug. My nervousness was increased by seeing how tall and heavily built he is in person. Rob introduced us and I shook Neil's hand, and to my surprise, he mentioned a couple of things that he knew about me (I guess Paul and Rob had told him), and the name of a mutual friend at Sabian, Chris Stankee, and smiled.

After catching up with Rob for a while, and chatting with me a little, Neil invited us onto the stage to watch the soundcheck. I was beyond excited. As he led us to the backstage area and over to his drumset, I looked around and remembered walking into Madison Square Garden with my father in 1984 (my very first rock concert), at 13 years old. Our seats were the absolute worst, in the top row of the arena, but I was transfixed by looking down at the beautiful red drums and gleaming cymbals.

Then Neil was suddenly motioning to me to climb up on the riser and take a seat on his drum throne. He walked around the kit and gave me a guided tour of the intricacies of his setup, we talked a little shop, and I was in heaven! Rob, knowing the significance of the occasion for me, walked around the kit and took photos of me with Neil. Soon Alex and Geddy emerged, and I asked Neil if I could stand behind him and watch him play the soundcheck, and he agreed. As I stood there watching him, I don't think my smile could have been any bigger.

As I watched the concert that evening, observing Neil playing some of my favorite songs once again, I saw him in an entirely different light. This day was a dream come true, something I will remember for the rest of my life. On the way home, my overriding feeling was a tremendous amount of gratitude to Rob and Paul for trusting me enough to bring me into this, and to Neil, who turned out to be gracious, charming, and friendly. If the whole story had ended there, I would have considered myself a really lucky guy. But after the soundcheck, as we said goodbye (although we had not talked about the project at all, interestingly), Neil shook my hand and said, "I'm looking forward to working with you." All along this entire process, I had tons of questions for Rob and Paul about whether they thought things were going well. As we walked back to our cars that evening, Rob told me that he felt really good about how things were proceeding.

The months came and went, our lives went on, Hudson put out a bunch of other products, and then suddenly, just as I began to assume this whole Neil project was probably never going to happen, Paul and Rob notified me that Neil was coming to New York to play in a Buddy Rich tribute concert (along with Chad Smith, Terry Bozzio, Tommy Igoe, John Blackwell, and others), and that he would make time to meet us for breakfast. On October 19, 2008, Paul and Rob and I met Neil at his hotel, and this time the agenda was to start hammering out the project. Neil had obviously spent time with my outline, but was not feeling enthusiastic about revisiting the older material. He respected my ideas, but explained that reexamining the past like that just wasn't interesting to him. In retrospect, my outline was wildly detailed, containing rare songs that he had not played for over ten years, and would have required a massive amount of research on his part into his past work. As we all poked at the remains of our pancakes, I began to feel the possibility of the project slipping away right there.

But another idea I had generated did catch Neil's interest. It was based around his own writing about the song "Far Cry," naming many of his influences on that drum part. I had called that theme "Connections," with the aim of using that song to explore the eclectic nature of Neil's drumming influences. As we continued to brainstorm, Neil agreed that he wanted to try to keep tweaking ideas until we nailed something that inspired him.

Following this meeting, we engaged in email exchanges over the course of several months, and Neil came up with the idea of basing the DVD on live performance. His first DVD, *A Work in Progress*, was about writing and recording the drum parts for a record. His second DVD, *Anatomy of a Drum Solo*, was about soloing. Neil thought the third DVD could cover the entire enterprise of preparing for a tour, and performing live: another area for which Neil is well known. In discussing live performance, we would need to show live performance, and that meant *Rush songs*—we would have the opportunity to discuss the details of his drum parts after all!

So we finally had it: a concept that would tie together my desire to get into the nuts and bolts, with something that was intellectually engaging and worthwhile to Neil. Only a few more dozen hours of tweaking the outline, and we would be in business!

Neil still had limited interest in going back and explaining the drum parts that he had made up decades ago. He was enthused about discussing how his style has developed, and even the actual parts, but not sitting there and breaking down an old fill note-for-note. So he came up with a possible solution: We could film him in his private drum rehearsals before the upcoming tour, thereby obtaining the demonstration footage we would need for all the songs to be discussed.

Neil shared with me the tentative setlist for the upcoming Time Machine tour, and I set about listing some points of discussion for each song. Now the stage was set . . .

The filming of *Taking Center Stage* was unlike any project I have ever worked on. The first bits were shot at Neil's rehearsals in May 2010, then we filmed an entire Rush concert in July 2010, and finally captured the speaking parts in January 2011. This required a massive degree of planning as to how the entire show would be cut together, which I did my best to organize as the months elapsed between the shoots. Along the way Neil, Rob, Paul and I would exchange ideas and notes on what we had filmed, so the program actually remained fluid all the way up until the editing stage. But in the end, the final program has come together in the most amazing way.

On May 5, 2010, Rob, Paul, and I, along with our director Gregory McKean, our longtime video engineer Dan Welch, and our veteran sound engineer, Sean McClintock, set off for California to meet up with Neil and film him in drum rehearsals at Drum Channel Studios in Oxnard, California, near the Drum Workshop factory. As we rolled past the fragrant strawberry fields nearby, and pulled up to the warehouse complex where Neil was working— like the president of some musical country engaged in secret work at an undisclosed location—my anticipation was building. We walked through the loading dock and past the stacks of DW boxes, then road cases stenciled with "Rush." Now Neil could be heard playing in the adjacent studio (for the record, he's one of the hardest hitters I have ever heard).

We immediately set to work filming Neil's rehearsals, as he played along to the recorded versions of each of the songs on the Time Machine setlist. We still didn't know how much exposition we would get from Neil at these sessions, because he had stressed that his main job was to prepare for the tour. So although the cameras were rolling and the machines were set to record, the actual content was still far from finalized. However, Neil surprised us right off the bat by speaking to the camera, and giving us wonderful explanations of his approach to rehearsals, as well as insights into the construction of his new drum solo.

The cameras documented Neil playing along to every song in the setlist, to be used as demonstration segments on the DVD. (In the final DVD, there is a ton of footage of Neil playing all of his classic parts by himself, and most of them are also presented in slow motion for easy analysis, accompanied by PDF transcriptions.) Over the three days, between sessions of playing, Neil sat with me before the cameras and discussed wide-ranging topics related to live performance, but the highlight for me came when he asked me to sit with him in the control room and listen to one of the new Rush songs, "Caravan." After sitting beside Neil in the studio to watch him play that song, we worked up some topics for discussion—resulting in an hour-long featurette about the creation of that drum part, entitled "The Story of 'Caravan.'"

On the last day, the obligatory lunch at In-N-Out Burger completed our successful trip to Southern California!

The next necessary step was to film Neil playing the songs live, which was accomplished July 23, 2010, at the Saratoga Performing Arts Center in Saratoga, New York. The footage we captured there is a dream come true for fans of Neil who want to observe and understand his playing: four separate cameras look at him from various angles, showing Neil only, playing every song in the setlist. We also created a special audio mix for the concert performances, with the drums turned up slightly louder than normal. This aspect of the DVD is unprecedented; not only do you get to see and hear Neil talk about and demonstrate the drum parts, but you also get to see the entire concert documented especially for drummers.

Capturing the live footage in Saratoga was challenging, yet fun. We arrived in the afternoon, and while the film crew documented the entire setup of Neil's kit (which is also included on the DVD), we met with Neil on the bus to discuss the plan for the day. Neil suggested we set up a camera in his dressing room right before showtime and film him warming up, along with a little "preamble." I scrambled to put together some notes for the interview, since I had not expected this.

As our cameras rolled, Neil discussed different topics related to live performance and soloing, and shared a lot of information about how he goes about his warmup, what he is thinking about during the warmup and show, and how he acquires new ideas even while warming up. I think viewers are really going to enjoy watching how relaxed Neil is in this interview, and seeing how much he still enjoys playing. His desire to continue to learn and grow as a drummer is inspirational.

On this particular day Neil also demonstrated his amazing professionalism. He had been combating an ear infection for a couple of weeks on the tour, to the point where one of his ears had almost completely closed up. A doctor arrived backstage to evaluate Neil's condition, and despite the fact that one of his ears was so clogged up that he could barely hear, Neil put on an amazing performance that night. We were also able to document the soundcheck, and that is also included on the DVD.

After the show, we set out for home satisfied with another successful expedition, this time capturing and documenting the activity of an entire day backstage at a Rush concert—along with the complete concert—from a drummer's perspective, for the first time ever.

By this point in the development and production process, all of us knew that we had something very special. Yet despite the fact that we had filmed rehearsals and demonstrations of the drum parts, the backstage scene, and all of the song performances, there was still something missing. The interviews we had done to this point covered topics related to live performance, but did not address the bread-and-butter questions I had prepared in my many outlines about the individual drum parts. We needed to get together for yet another shoot, so Neil could actually discuss the songs.

From the outset, Neil wanted to do this in a spectacular natural setting, preferably outdoors, to give the show a cinematic quality, and give the viewer a break from the studio and stage environments of the performances. Several locations were discussed as we began to compare schedules, but we were looking at a window of available time in Neil's calendar that put us smack in the middle of winter. Neil suggested Death Valley National Park as a suitable location, for its great natural beauty, and because the chances of rain spoiling the shoot were practically nil. Rob, Paul, and I were going to be in Southern California in January for the NAMM show anyway, so it was settled—we would rendezvous in Death Valley.

After flying into Las Vegas late at night, Paul, Rob, and I set out early the next morning, heading across the desert toward Death Valley—one of the most memorable and incredible experiences of my life. Of course I had read about and seen photos of Death Valley, but as with viewing any natural wonder, important piece of architecture, or famous painting, nothing compares to seeing it with your own eyes. From the moment we drove into the park, the breathtaking vistas and unbelievable colors had us all commenting to each other about how spectacular everything looked.

Armed with our map (cell phone and GPS signals don't reach the area too well, which actually adds to the spirit of adventure of visiting the place), we drove through some scenic mountain and desert areas and finally found our way to the Furnace Creek Inn, where Neil had arrived the previous night. The Inn is a date-palm oasis, a green jewel in the barren, brown desert. The low-slung building is set halfway into the side of a mountain, and was built early in the 20th century, with scenic terraces and red tile roofs framing the formal dining room and windowed lobby. You could spend a couple of days just exploring the Inn itself. But after a very quick lunch with Neil, we mapped out a plan of attack for the next two days of shooting. Neil reviewed the questions and topics I had proposed as discussion points, added some tweaks and changes of his own, and we narrowed the topics down to focus on the truly unique and essential elements of each song's drum part. The Hudson crew piled into our vehicles, and Neil mounted his motorcycle. Knowing the park well, Neil first led us to the general store and gas station in Furnace Creek, where everyone stocked up on snacks and drinks to get them through the day.

Then we headed for Artist's Palette and Zabriskie Point, two vistas in the park that look like paintings made real. The desert presents a fantastic mosaic of colors that is completely unexpected until you experience it. As we began to capture footage of Neil discussing his drum parts in front of these breathtaking scenes, we realized that his idea of juxtaposing the timeless serenity of this natural setting with the lights and loud excitement of the concert was brilliant. As we proceeded with the filming, I was (along with Neil, it seemed) truly enjoying talking about his work on songs such as "Subdivisions," "Free Will," "Far Cry," and so many more.

As the light faded on the first day, we headed across the park to our hotel, located in a small village (actually more like a cluster of buildings) called Stovepipe Wells. To give you an idea of the scale of Death Valley, it took us over an hour to drive the two-lane road from Zabriskie Point to Stovepipe Wells. The motel was a compound of one-story, dark brown Western-style clapboard buildings, perfectly suited to the landscape—overlooking one of the only areas with actual sand dunes in Death Valley National Park (most of the landscape is rocky, not sandy). A cluster of mesquite trees overhung the restaurant, bar, and small common room at the center of the complex. When I entered my room, I immediately noticed there was no TV, no phone, and no clock. Perfect!

We relied on our cell phones (though they had no phone service) to check the time and set wake-up alarms each morning. After a fun dinner at the restaurant with the entire crew, including Neil, all sitting at a long table, eating together and sharing stories, I couldn't resist the temptation to walk about a half mile down the road, and then a few hundred yards off to the side of it, just to experience the dark of the desert. I have never seen that many stars in the sky, and I have never experienced that kind of enveloping blackness. What an amazing experience. I don't know if there is anything out there that could have possibly attacked me, but I figured I would head back to my room before I found out.

The second day of filming captured scenic footage of Neil riding along various park roads on his motorcycle, majestic scenes that would all be pieced together in the final program to create a movie-like quality. We headed to an area called the Natural Bridge, which involved a hike up a canyon to reach a bridge-like geological formation carved out by water. By this point Neil and I had done enough interviews that our exchanges became more conversational and more fun, as so often happens with two enthusiastic drummers talking about their craft. Rob, who had gone back to the general store to pick up lunch for everyone, returned as we headed back down the canyon to the cars. Seeing Rob hiking toward us like an overladen pack mule, Neil and I both grabbed a few items to help him out as we headed down the hill. One of my favorite photos from the trip is of Neil and me walking down the hill together, smiling and carrying bags of potato chips and pretzels. Neil gave that shot the perfect title: "Snack Boys."

After lunch we continued down the snaking main park road to Badwater Basin, the lowest, driest, and hottest spot in North America. (Luckily, it was January, when it wasn't so hot. I can only imagine what it must be like in summer, when temperatures can reach 120 degrees and more—the record is 138. It can truly be a life-threatening environment.)

After parking along the road overlooking the basin, we finally got a closer look at the salt flats we had been admiring from higher up. A rare rain had left a couple of inches of water in the center of the basin, making it look like a lake. Death Valley typically receives less than two inches of rain per year, and its surfaces are hard and impermeable, so a little moisture can linger for a while. As the water evaporates, it leaves behind the signature white color of the salt flats.

We decided we would get closer to the water so that the "lake" would be in the background behind Neil, with the mountains reflected on the surface. But as we walked out and downward toward the salt flat, we discovered that the evaporating water not only leaves behind white salt, it also leaves nice, deep mud. All of us began sinking up to our ankles as we tried to find the proper location to shoot. The crew had some two-by-fours, which Neil and the camera could stand on, and we were able to get what we needed. Fortunately none of us was swallowed by quicksand—although Dan came close.

From Badwater, at 282 feet below sea level, we could look up the sheer cliff face toward our next and final destination, Dante's View—at an elevation of 5,475 feet. Although not more than a mile or so above us, the only way by vehicle would take us back to Furnace Creek, then slowly up the winding mountain road to the overlook point at the top. This trip would take us at least an hour, and the park ranger who had been supervising our shoot told us that snow had covered the road near the top, and it was closed by a locked gate. He thought maybe he could get us up there in his 4x4, perhaps with Greg's crew in their Suburban, but our sedan and Neil's motorcycle would be out of luck. Neil told us he would stop for gas in Furnace Creek, then meet us at the closed gate to wait for the ranger.

Paul, Rob, and I drove along for over an hour, passing the Inn at about the halfway point, and noticing the temperature getting gradually colder as we ascended into higher elevations. The road began to climb steeply, with signs pointing towards Dante's View. We noticed little patches of snow on the ground, and came to the gate the ranger had told us about—but it was open, and none of the other guys were around. We parked by the side of the road and waited. After about thirty minutes, there was still no sign of anyone. Surely the ranger would have come down to get us if things were safe by now, wouldn't he? And Neil said he had to stop for gas. Was he behind us or ahead of us? Without cell phone service, there was no way of knowing if he had attempted the snowy pass above, or even if he had fallen and been injured. Adding to all of this, the sun was beginning to get low in the sky, threatening to leave us without the final bits of shooting we needed. After another ten minutes we decided to go on ahead and see what had happened. As we neared the summit, slippery patches of snow covered the road. None of us being motorcycle riders ourselves, these patches looked much too dangerous for a bike to cross.

But Neil had just kept riding, tiptoeing through those snowy patches as far as the summit—all the while expecting to encounter a closed gate. Then, he wondered why no one else was there. Eventually Greg, Dan, and the guys followed him up in the Suburban, and captured some terrific shots of Neil riding up the final switchbacks of the road and pulling into the overlook at Dante's View.

As we rode up, we saw that not only was everyone okay, but they were framing the final scene, just as we were beginning to lose light. Right on the precipice of Dante's View sat Neil on his bike, while below him lay a stunning panorama of the whole of Death Valley. Here, as the sunset turned golden, Neil filmed the introduction to the entire DVD, on the last minute of the last day of the shoot, in which he summarized all the work that been done in the days, weeks and months before.

As soon as Greg called, "That's a wrap," Neil expressed concern about riding down through the icy passes, and immediately set off. The rest of us gathered our stuff and followed, while Greg and Dan stayed behind for a few minutes to capture the sun slipping down behind the Panamint Mountains across the valley. As Paul, Rob, and I descended in our car and finally came back down to the parts of the mountainside that were free of frost, we saw Neil sitting by the side of the road on his bike. Pulling up alongside, we rolled down the window to see if anything was wrong.

"Oh no," he said, "just enjoying the moment."

Then we could see that at this vantage point, the golden dusk had bathed the sky in all purple and pink, but still allowed a beautiful multicolored view of miles and miles of Death Valley and its surrounding mountains spread out below us. Neil smiled, and we left him with his thoughts and continued back to Stovepipe Wells.

That night we gathered for a final dinner, all of us sitting at the same long table. The occasion called for an extra glass of wine for all of us (which Neil added on top of, I suspect, a private Macallan or two in his room). Interestingly, Neil and I had both battled colds during the entire shoot, and one of our cameramen, Jeff, had experienced a serious bout of food poisoning on the first day, yet after the incredible experiences we had shared together over the past two days, all of this was forgotten as we talked and laughed. When our drinks arrived, Neil raised his glass to toast and thank all of us, and to say that this trip and shoot was one of the most wonderful experiences of his life. I glanced at Paul and Rob, and saw that they were as deeply moved as I was.

Well, after the brief encounter of the next morning which I described at the beginning of the story, we had pretty much reached the end of the exciting stuff. Neil went back out on tour with Rush, and I delved into the post-production process with our longtime editor Phil Fallo and veteran sound engineer Sean McClintock, both of whom put in countless hours on this project. With Paul and Rob overseeing each step, I called in our longtime transcription and engraving assistant Willie Rose to help with the PDFs, and communicated regularly with Hudson's Al Giordano, the unsung hero who gets all the important yet uncelebrated details of projects together for us, from booking flights and arranging shoot locations to getting printing and design templates and specifications for the packaging, and countless other important details. (And I must mention that Neil loves Al's dry New York wit.) It is pretty much all careening towards the finish line at this point.

Having viewed the nearly seven hours of the final program, cut together in breathtaking fashion by Phil, I truly believe that this is one of the most incredible drum DVDs ever made. The bulk of the program consists of the songs and the show, and it is amazing to see how segments of video that were shot in three different locations over the course of a year have come together in such a perfect way. Each song has its own chapter, which begins with Neil in Death Valley discussing the specific details of the drum grooves and fills contained in the song. For each of these grooves or fills, there is an accompanying drums-only demonstration (from his rehearsals), both in real time and in slow motion, that clearly allows the viewer to see everything that Neil is doing. Each of these demonstrations is also accompanied by a transcription and an included PDF that is keyed with on-screen icons for clear identification. Once Neil has discussed and analyzed all of the sections of the song, we watch him perform the song in concert in Saratoga, seen from only the drum cameras, and with the special audio mix I described above (with the drums turned up). I guess I can sum it up by saying that when I was a kid, I wished there was a video that showed all of this. As it turns out, I can't believe I got to help make it.

I can't thank Neil enough for trusting me to work on this project with him, and for the respect he has shown for my work as a player, editor, and educator. It has been a thrill and an honor to spend some time with him. I hope that this DVD will be an educational and motivational experience for everyone who watches it. Thanks to Neil's ability to explain and discuss his ideas in such articulate and detailed terms, I think this DVD will be hugely interesting not only to drummers, but to all Rush fans, and even people who are simply curious about an examination of the creative process—presented in a uniquely scenic and eloquent fashion.

Finally, I sincerely thank my two bosses, Rob Wallis and Paul Siegel of Hudson Music, for making one of my dreams come true. What an unbelievable journey it has been.

I can't wait for everyone to see this thing! If, like me, you ever wore out a copy of *Exit…Stage Left* as a kid, I think you're going to be pretty amazed.

Joe Bergamini
Whippany, NJ
July 2011

DRUM KEY

CHAPTER 1

   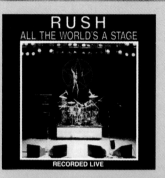

Following the release of their self-titled debut album, Rush found themselves looking for a drummer after the departure of John Rutsey. Neil Peart auditioned and got the gig in 1974, and for the next six years the band toured and recorded nearly nonstop. The years 1975-77 saw Rush release three studio albums, followed by their first live record, *All the World's a Stage*. This intense period of work allowed the entire band to develop their technical performance and songwriting skills very quickly. From the very beginning, Neil established himself as a creative player with an equal role in the band, and not just a background drummer. Although his playing achieved a much more complex level as the years progressed, the albums *Fly by Night*, *Caress of Steel*, and *2112* each contain the

trademark energy, intelligence, and creativity that would make Neil celebrated among drummers. The drum solo on *All the World's a Stage* is interesting to hear, since it contains certain elements that Neil would soon abandon, yet also includes signature elements that would stay with him.

A set of maple-shelled, chrome-finished Slingerlands were the first drums Neil used in Rush, which he bought from a music store in Toronto shortly after joining the band. Neil used this set from 1974-77, and it can be heard on the albums *Fly by Night*, *Caress of Steel*, *2112*, and the live album *All the World's a Stage* (where the bass drums were recorded without front heads and with heavy muffling). According to Neil, he did not set out specifically to look for Slingerland drums, but fell in love with the kit when he saw it at the store. For Neil's first two tours with the band (the ones that supported the albums *Rush* and *Fly by Night*), this kit was used, but did not yet include the four concert toms or any of the percussion instruments, and lacked one of the 16" crash cymbals. The concert toms were added for the *Caress of Steel* tour, while the percussion instruments were added for the *2112* tour. This drumset was retired in 1977 and replaced by a new set of Slingerlands for the *A Farewell to Kings* album and tour.

It is interesting to note the sizes of the drums on this kit; they are different from what Neil settled on later. There were two 13" toms, for one thing, and the largest mounted tom, floor tom, and bass drums were different sizes (14", 16", 22") from what Neil played for many years after this (15", 18", 24"). The cymbal sizes chosen at this time, however, remained remarkably consistent (only the splashes later changed to larger sizes), and the 22" Zildjian Ping Ride in particular stayed with with Neil for many later albums and tours. This kit lacks any China cymbals, and the percussion setup is quite small compared to what was to come. Interestingly, it seems that on the *2112* tour, Neil played the orchestra bells away from the kit, near the side of the stage. They would soon be integrated into the kit beneath the concert toms, which is where they would stay. (The acoustic orchestra bells were replaced in the mid-1980s with a MalletKAT electronic percussion controller.)

Despite the above differences, however, by the time 1976 rolled around, Neil had settled on a basic arrangement of the drums and cymbals that he wouldn't really change much for twenty years. Also, with this kit he acquired the Slingerland Artist snare drum that would be his standby until his switch to DW drums in 1995. This drum had a three-ply shell which vintage drum collectors identify as being composed of maple/poplar/mahogany, with maple reinforcement rings. Neil has stated in many interviews that he purchased the drum second-hand for $60, and that the previous owner had modified the bearing edges—and this modification contributed to the drum's extreme dynamic range and unique sound. Originally finished with a copper-colored wrap, this snare was refinished many times over the years to match Neil's current kit.

Most of the hardware on this set was by Slingerland, although Neil did use Ludwig Speed King pedals at this time. He continued to do so until 1982, when he switched to Tama Camco pedals. His choice of drumsticks in 1976 was the Pro-Mark 747 Rock model; not only does Neil still use this model, but it now bears his name (as part of Pro-Mark's "Signature" series).

The first time Rush published a tour program was on the *2112* tour, but it did not yet include information about the band's equipment, so there are no direct quotes available here from Neil about this particular setup.

After Neil retired them, these Slingerland drums eventually found their way into the hands of a collector, who displayed them in the early 2000s at the Percussive Arts Society International Convention (PASIC), where fans posed for pictures with them.

DRUM SETUP

Drums:	Cymbals:	Percussion:

Slingerland in Chrome finish

1. 14x22 bass drum
2. 5.5x14 "Old Faithful" Slingerland Artist snare drum
3. 5.5x6 concert tom
4. 5.5x8 concert tom
5. 6.5x10 concert tom
6. 8x12 concert tom
7. 9x13 tom
8. 9x13 tom
9. 10x14 tom
10. 16x16 floor tom

Zildjian

A. 13" New Beat Hi-Hats
B. 20" Medium Crash
C. 16" Medium Crash
D. 8" Splash
E. 16" Medium Crash
F. 6" Splash
G. 22" Ping Ride
H. 18" Medium Crash

aa. orchestra bells (glockenspiel) (not included in kit; played near side of stage)
bb. cowbells
cc. "cluster" chimes/wind chimes
dd. wind chimes (bar chimes)

CHAPTER 2

A Farewell to Kings Tour

(1977)

A *Farewell to Kings* is packed with fantastic drumming, the complexity and creativity of which takes a major leap from Neil's previous studio performances with Rush. As their musicality improved with constant touring, the band created more challenging compositions. In fact, there are two songs on *A Farewell to Kings* that contain arguably some of the most difficult odd-meter passages in the entire Rush catalog: "A Farewell to Kings" and "Cygnus X-1" both use multiple odd meters contained within complex song arrangements. The album also contains tasteful, grooving drumming on "Closer to the Heart" and "Madrigal," powerful rock energy on "Cinderella Man," and intellectual art-rock playing on "Xanadu." It is clear that by 1977, with this album and tour, Neil's technical ability and conceptual approach to the drumset were advancing at an incredibly rapid pace.

For *A Farewell to Kings* and *Hemispheres*, and the tours that followed them, in 1977 Neil switched to a new Slingerland drumset, with five-ply maple shells, black and silver Niles badges, and "Blakrome" (a kind of reflective black) finish. The sizes of the drums and basic configuration would not change again until the mid-1990s, when Neil began to study with Freddie Gruber. In the tour program for *A Farewell to Kings*, for the first time, all three members of Rush included an equipment list, probably realizing that a large percentage of their audience was comprised of musicians. This gives us a special insight into what Neil was thinking as his setup changed through the years. Geddy and Alex have long since turned their tour program equipment list pages into a space for jokes, while Neil continues to write seriously about each new drumset on each tour—because he, like most drummers, loves to talk shop.

It was around this time that Neil began to expand the percussion voices on his kit, as Rush began to include more progressive and symphonic influences in their music. On *A Farewell to Kings*, the orchestra bells and chimes can be heard on "Closer to the Heart," and every percussion instrument shown in the diagram gets used in "Xanadu." Neil also added a pair of timbales, which are heard on "Xanadu" and the album's title track, and which became an important part of his voice on the next few albums.

Neil also added to his cymbal setup for this album and tour, incorporating for the first time a Chinese cymbal: a 20-inch Zildjian Pang with rivets. Otherwise, his selection of cymbals and drumsticks remained consistent. At this time he was using Remo C.S. Dot batter heads on the snare drum, toms, and bass drums, and Evans heads on the bottom of his toms. He continued to use mixed brands of drumheads for many years.

From the A Farewell to Kings tour book, Neil writes:

My drums are all by Slingerland, with the shells all treated with a process called vibra-fibing, which puts a thin layer of fiberglass on the inner shell. This helps to improve the natural warmth and resonance of the drums, while it sharpens the attack to give greater projection. The kit consists of two 24" bass drums, 6", 8", 10", and 12" concert toms, 12", 13", 15", and 18" closed toms, and a 5"x14" wooden snare drum. The cymbals are all by Avedis Zildjian: a 6" and 8" splash, two 16", one 18", and one 20" crash cymbals, a 22" ride, an 18" pang, and a pair of 13" hi-hats.

My collection of percussion "toys" currently includes tubular bells, glockenspiel, wind chimes, temple blocks, timbales, bell tree, triangles, and a set of melodic cowbells. I use Remo C.S. Black Dot drumheads on my snare and bass drums, Ludwig Silver Dots on the concert toms and timbales, and Evans Looking Glass (top) and blue Hydraulic (bottom) on the tom-toms. I use Pro-Mark 747 drumsticks, with the varnish sanded off of the gripping area.

DRUM SETUP

Drums:

Slingerland in "Blakrome" finish, with the inside of shells vibra-fibed

1. 14x24 bass drum
2. 5.5x14 "Old Faithful" Slingerland Artist snare drum
3. 5.5x6 concert tom
4. 5.5x8 concert tom
5. 6.5x10 concert tom
6. 8x12 concert tom
7. 8x12 tom
8. 9x13 tom
9. 12x15 tom
10. 16x18 floor tom
11. 6.5x13 Slingerland brass timbale
12. 6.5x14 Slingerland brass timbale

Cymbals:

Zildjian

A. 13" New Beat Hi-Hats
B. 20" Medium Crash
C. 16" Medium Crash
D. 8" Splash
E. 16" Medium Crash
F. 6" Splash
G. 22" Ping Ride
H. 18" Medium Crash
I. 18" Pang

Percussion:

aa. orchestra bells (glockenspiel)
bb. triangle
cc. bell tree
dd. cowbells
ee. wind chimes (bar chimes)
ff. "cluster" chimes/wind chimes
gg. temple blocks
hh. chimes (tubular bells)

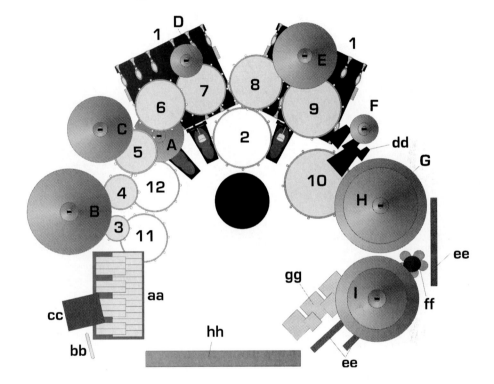

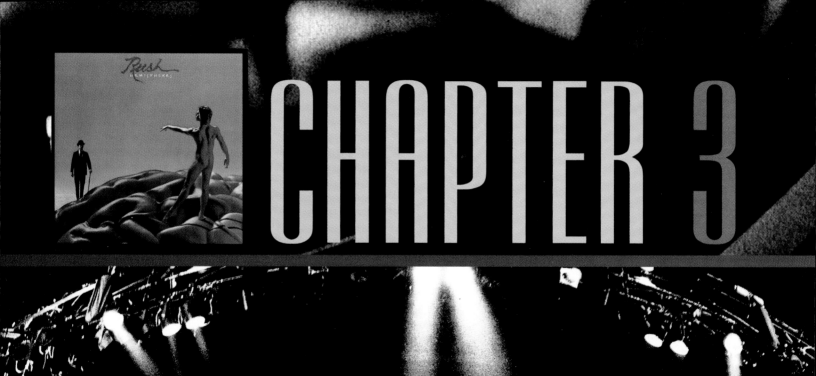

CHAPTER 3

Hemispheres is an album that many Rush fans consider to be a classic. It is certainly a monumental achievement in terms of the complexity and architecture of its drum parts. As Neil continued to develop new layers of complexity in his playing, his setup continued to grow. Most of the new additions were made in the percussion department, where Neil added gong, pipe chimes, timpani, crotales, more triangles, new temple blocks, and more bar chimes. He had effectively become a one-man orchestral percussion section!

While the cymbal setup stayed relatively consistent, there were a couple of key additions: a 20" Zildjian Swish and an 18" Wuhan Chinese. Neil was one of the first well-known Western drummers to incorporate the Wuhan cymbal, which was actually made in China. The aggressive sound and short attack of this cymbal made it possible to play tighter rhythmic patterns, such as playing it on every upbeat of the bar in a groove. Neil put this new sound to great use, employing it as a groove device in many classic Rush tunes.

The drums themselves were the same maple-shelled Slingerlands that Neil used on the *A Farewell to Kings* tour. This was, by the way, the first drumset that Neil had "vibra-fibed," which was a proprietary process performed by The Percussion Center in Fort Wayne, Indiana, that involved placing a thin layer of fiberglass on the inside of each shell. Neil felt that this improved the attack of his drums. Although Larry Allen, who was Neil's drum tech at the time, worked at The Percussion Center, the actual custom work on Neil's drums and hardware was done by the owner of the store, Neal Graham, who went on to found XL Specialty Percussion, a company that specialized in drum cases and marching percussion hardware. Neal, a very creative individual, is still active in the percussion industry today as a consultant, having sold XL Specialty to Gator Cases. It was Neal who did the vibra-fibing of the shells, brass plating of the hardware, and customization of the cymbal stands on all of Neil's drumsets up until he switched to DW.

From the Hemispheres tour book, Neil writes:

My drums are all by Slingerland, with the inner surface of the wooden shells treated with a process called vibra-fibing. This consists of a thin layer of glass fiber and resin placed on the inside of the shell. The drums consist of two 24" bass drums, 6", 8", 10", and 12" concert toms, 12", 13", 15", and 18" tom-toms, and a 5"x14" wood-shell snare drum. All cymbals are by Avedis Zildjian, with the exception of an 18" Chinese cymbal. The Zildjians are 6" and 8" splash, two 16", one 18" and one 20" crash cymbals, a 22" ride, a pair of 13" hi-hats, 18" pang, and a 20" China type. In the percussion department are orchestra bells, tubular bells, wind chimes, crotales, timbales, tympani, gong, temple blocks, bell tree, triangle, and melodic cowbells. For heads I use Remo Black Dots on the snare and bass drums, Ludwig Silver Dots on the concert toms and timbales, and Evans Looking Glass (top) and blue Hydraulic (bottom) on the closed toms. My hardware consists of Ludwig Speed King pedals, and Tama and Pearl stands. I use Pro-Mark 747 drumsticks with the varnish sanded off the gripping area.

DRUM SETUP

Drums:

Slingerland in "Blakrome" finish, with the inside of shells vibra-fibed (except timpani)

1. 14x24 bass drum
2. 5.5x14 "Old Faithful" Slingerland Artist snare drum
3. 5.5x6 concert tom
4. 5.5x8 concert tom
5. 6.5x10 concert tom
6. 8x12 concert tom
7. 8x12 tom
8. 9x13 tom
9. 12x15 tom
10. 16x18 floor tom
11. timpani
12. 6.5x13 Slingerland brass timbale
13. 6.5x14 Slingerland brass timbale

Cymbals:

Zildjian (except Wuhan)

A. 13" New Beat Hi-Hats
B. 20" Medium Crash
C. 16" Medium Crash
D. 8" Splash
E. 16" Medium Crash
F. 6" Splash
G. 22" Ping Ride
H. 18" Medium Crash
I. 20" Swish
J. 18" Wuhan Chinese
K. 18" Pang

Percussion:

aa. orchestra bells (glockenspiel)
bb. bell tree
cc. wind chimes (bar chimes)
dd. triangles
ee. cowbells
ff. temple blocks
gg. large chimes
hh. gong
ii. chimes (tubular bells)
jj. crotales

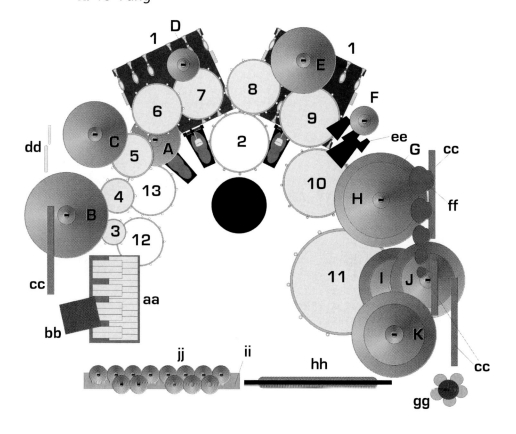

Hemispheres (1978) is considered a seminal progressive rock album. Along with *A Farewell to Kings* (1977), this is the closest Rush ever got to the "art rock" of bands like Gentle Giant, early Genesis, and Yes. During this time period, Rush expanded its use of odd time signatures, pushing themselves to play the most difficult parts they could handle, and employed a wide range of dynamics and textures, sometimes in longer song formats.

Hemispheres is one of the Rush albums referenced often by drummers as a "must-have," and it is easy to see why. The entire album is a front-to-back tour de force of extremely creative and challenging drumming. The constant touring and recording from the time of his joining Rush had sharpened Neil's skills in just about every area, and by the time they recorded *Hemispheres*, Neil was bursting with new ideas and tools to put to use.

"The Trees" is one of only four tracks on *Hemispheres* (the title track is 20 minutes long), and contains an interesting arrangement with an unconventional song form. There is a 4/4 verse in the beginning of the song that returns again at the end, but in between, the song goes into another "verse" in 6/8, followed by a quiet interlude and aggressive guitar solo in 5/4. Although there is no standard "verse-chorus" form to follow, the song is an exquisite composition that is both catchy and musical despite being a bit unusual.

ANALYSIS:

This performance of "The Trees" is a bonus song on the *Taking Center Stage* DVD (disc 3), which was filmed on the *Snakes & Arrows* tour. Neil chose to play this song on his Roland V-Drum kit, which allowed him to play the percussion instruments recorded on the original version using samples on the V-Drums and MalletKAT. The sounds that Neil triggers on the electronic kit include the temple blocks, bell tree, wind chimes (all on V-Drum pads), and orchestra bells (on the MalletKAT). The only acoustic percussion instruments on Neil's current kit are the cowbells, which are also used here.

Although Neil uses all electronic sounds on this performance, it has been notated with the same standard drum key as the rest of the book, since the drum sounds triggered are the same voices as would have been played on the acoustic kit. For the temple blocks and cowbells, the use of the particular instrument is indicated in a text note above the staff, and a diamond-shaped notehead has been used, with the relative pitches of those instruments shown on the staff.

One of the most interesting aspects of "The Trees" is the way it shifts meters. On the DVD, the song fades up at the end of the acoustic guitar introduction. The beginning section is in 6/8, with an eighth-note rate of 138 BPM. This converts to the quarter-note pulse on the loud band entrance, and you can hear Neil loudly count "three, four, five, six" as he counts the band in with stick clicks. The drum part starts with the first of several full-kit crescendo/build-up rhythms. From the electronic kit, Neil can easily reach his large 18" mounted tom, and he uses this drum in measures 4 and 6 (and throughout the song) for these sections.

At measure 19, the song shifts back to 6/8 time, and the quarter-note pulse becomes the eighth note in 6/8, taking the song back to the approximate tempo of the guitar-and-vocal intro. The groove in this section of the song resembles a standard blues groove, but with fills and figures occurring throughout. There is an odd bar at measure 37, which has been expressed as a bar of 4/8, before the long tom roll leading to the interlude. It seemed to make the most sense to feel the shortened measure there, and then count the long tom roll as a bar of 6/8.

THE TREES

After the temple-block interlude, the guitars shift to 5/4 and this section builds into the guitar solo. Starting at measure 69, Neil plays interesting syncopations around the guitar melody, and then breaks into a straighter feel at measure 77 (which is the where the guitar solo actually enters). Notice that Neil plays beats 1 and 2 on the snare drum in this section, which has an effect of smoothing out the 5/4. Most drummers would double up the snare on 4 and 5, which has an angular feeling and matches the time, but the way Neil does it actually carries the momentum into the next bar and smooths out the odd number of beats in the bar.

The song shifts into 3/4 at measure 84 for some tricky band unisons with cowbell figures, then back to 5/4 before ultimately resolving into 4/4 at measure 103, which is the reprise of the verse section (measure 7). All in all, "The Trees" qualifies as a prog-rock masterpiece!

THE TREES

THE TREES

THE TREES

Cowbells:

Wind chime sample:

Improvise on MalletKat, blocks and chimes to fade:

Neil refers to this song as "our all-time most self-indulgent instrumental," which is probably true, and it's not like that's a bad thing! "La Villa Strangiato" is the second song in this package taken from the *Hemispheres* album, and is one of the most legendary Rush songs of all time. The original version clocks in at over nine minutes, and although the *Taking Center Stage* version is truncated, it is still one of the longer songs on the DVD. It is absolutely bursting with all of the characteristics that have made Rush some of the most respected rock musicians of all time: creative and memorable parts, multiple odd time signatures, high-energy rock playing, inventive dynamics, and (of course) plenty of challenging drum grooves and fills.

For the Time Machine tour, the arrangement of the song was edited slightly from the original version, essentially by removing the repeats on some of the parts that recur through the song. In addition, in order to spice things up a bit, the band added a comical polka intro, in which Neil plays a bell melody on the MalletKAT. This melody has been written out the first time it occurs, but is played a few more times during the intro.

Some other interesting items to watch for in this song are the nice range of dynamics between the aggressive main theme and the 7/8 interlude section, the creative drum breaks and fills, and the extensive use of ghost notes throughout the tune.

ANALYSIS:

The new polka intro ends at measure 25, where the band launches into the familiar main theme of the song. Pay careful attention to the many hi-hat openings here, because they are very important to making the groove feel right. At measure 37, Neil uses his signature ride pattern. The original version of "La Villa" (on *Hemispheres*) was the first time Neil ever used this pattern. At measure 63, the song shifts into 7/8 time (notice that this section repeats three times), and the pattern that is played here is a kind of bridge between the main theme and the upcoming groove in the guitar interlude.

The 7/8 guitar interlude begins at measure 68, using this creative little groove as its main theme. As the section develops, Neil drops in different hi-hat openings in various places. Starting at the end of measure 102, the dynamic begins to build, and Neil introduces a syncopated variation on the 7/8 groove theme. After building for several more bars, a one-bar fill leads down to a funky ghost-note groove that percolates along and builds, introducing the China cymbal, and eventually reaches a climax at the loud groove in measure 142.

"Monsters!" is the name of the section that begins at measure 146. This section (still in 7/8) features a heavy guitar theme with a "tribal tom" treatment on the drums, incorporating the larger toms and China cymbal. There's also quite a bit of left-foot action here. Coming out of this theme, at measure 158, during Geddy's bass solo, Neil plays an eighth-and-two-sixteenths rhythm with his right hand on the ride cymbal, and fills in a couple of tasty hi-hat openings and snare-drum accents with his left hand. The entire next section of the song, from measures 160-176, is jammed with challenging unison figures played by the entire band, with Neil filling the space in between on his ride or hi-hat. In the middle of all this, in measures 167-168, there are two interesting drum fills. Note that the band accents the "&" of beat 4 in bar 167, and beat 1 in bar 168, so these fills sound like two separate one-bar ideas, since Neil is catching the band figures in between. The first of these fills contains fast sixteenth-note triplets, and the second is an interesting accent pattern on the toms with some quick double bass dropped in.

Neil plays one of his most exciting solo drum breaks at measure 177, displaying fast singles around the entire kit, mixed with a couple of well-placed hi-hat barks. The placement of the accents in the first part of this break is what makes it sound so cool, so carefully study the DVD (or original recording) until you understand how this pattern is articulated. This drum break leads into a relatively sparse groove in 4/4 that has a very interesting lope to it. The main snare drum and bass drum accents in this pattern follow the guitar melody, and show how syncopation on the drums can enhance the feel and character of a section of music, and not just play a supportive role.

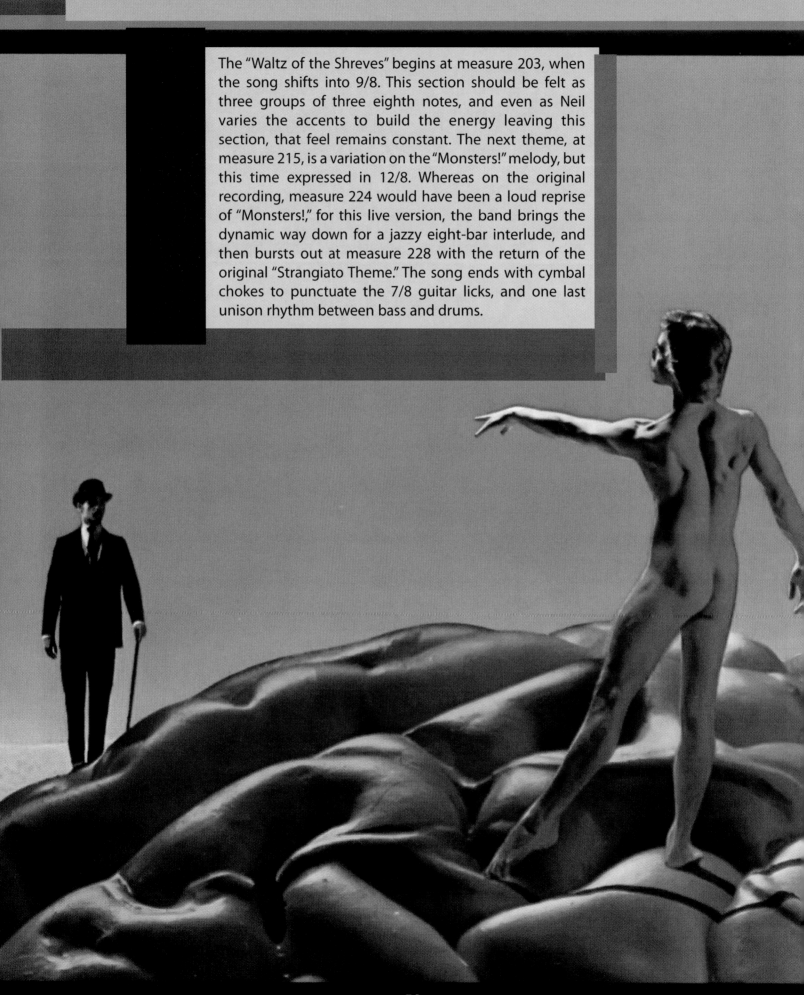

The "Waltz of the Shreves" begins at measure 203, when the song shifts into 9/8. This section should be felt as three groups of three eighth notes, and even as Neil varies the accents to build the energy leaving this section, that feel remains constant. The next theme, at measure 215, is a variation on the "Monsters!" melody, but this time expressed in 12/8. Whereas on the original recording, measure 224 would have been a loud reprise of "Monsters!," for this live version, the band brings the dynamic way down for a jazzy eight-bar interlude, and then bursts out at measure 228 with the return of the original "Strangiato Theme." The song ends with cymbal chokes to punctuate the 7/8 guitar licks, and one last unison rhythm between bass and drums.

LA VILLA STRANGIATO

LA VILLA STRANGIATO

LA VILLA STRANGIATO

LA VILLA STRANGIATO

LA VILLA STRANGIATO

LA VILLA STRANGIATO

LA VILLA STRANGIATO

CHAPTER 4

PERMANENT WAVES TOUR
(1979-80)

This album and tour marked the beginning of Neil's relationship with Tama. His use of Tama drums at the point in his career when he became a worldwide drum icon was of enormous benefit to Tama, fueling sales of thousands of Superstar drumsets. While the shells and hardware of this drumset were the same specifications as was available to the public, Neil had the drums highly customized: the inside of the shells were vibra-fibed, all the hardware was brass-plated, and the finish was a custom rosewood color that Neil wanted to duplicate from some Chinese furniture that he had acquired. All of the custom work was again performed by Neal Graham at The Percussion Center in Fort Wayne, Indiana. From this time forward, all of Neil's drumsets would be highly customized, just like (as Neil likes to say) the custom "dream cars" at auto shows.

Regular drummers had to settle for what in stock at their local shop. The closest color choice available to the public on Tama Superstar drums in the 1980s was "Cherry Wine" (a red stain finish), and this became the most popular finish thanks to Neil's influence.

With this kit, Neil received a matching snare drum from Tama, but chose to keep his 5.5x14 Slingerland "Artist" model snare, which was soon to become known as "Old Faithful." For the rest of the kit, the sizes of the new Tama drums matched the sizes of Neil's old Slingerland kit exactly.

On this tour Neil was still using the extensive percussion setup from the *Hemispheres* tour, including a timpani and gong. The setlist on the *Permanent Waves* tour included long, progressive songs such as "Xanadu," "Jacob's Ladder," and "The Trees," which feature extensive percussion, as well as "Cygnus X-1," "Natural Science," "La Villa Strangiato," and abbreviated versions of "Hemispheres" and "By-Tor and the Snow Dog." Many of these longer songs would soon be retired from live performance, some temporarily and some permanently.

From the Permanent Waves tour book, Neil writes:

I recently became the proud owner of a new set of Tama drums, once again with the inner side of the wooden shells coated with the vibra-fibing treatment. Along with the custom finish and the brass-plated metal hardware, this operation was performed by The Percussion Center of Fort Wayne, Indiana. The sizes of the drums remain unchanged, consisting of two 24" bass drums, 6", 8", 10", and 12" concert toms, 12", 13" 15", and 18" closed toms, and a 5-1/2" x 14" wooden snare drum. I probably need hardly add that both on the road, and most especially on this newest record, I am very pleased with the combination of the thick, wooden shells, and the dependable, modern hardware. All my cymbals are still by Avedis Zildjian, with the exception of one 18" Chinese cymbal. They are a 6" and 8" splash, two 16", one 18", and one 20" crash cymbals, a 22" ride, a pair of 13" hi-hats, an 18" pang, and a 20" China type. Digging into the toy box we find the usual assortment of effects, including timbales, melodic cowbells, orchestra bells, wind chimes, tubular bells, bell tree, tympani, temple blocks, triangle, gong, and crotales. On my snare and bass drums I use Remo Black Dot heads, Ludwig Silver Dots on the concert toms, and Evans Looking Glass (top) and blue Hydraulic (bottom) on the other toms. Ludwig Speed King pedals and Tama hardware complete the setup. My drumsticks are still Pro-Mark 747s with the varnish removed from the gripping area.

DRUM SETUP

Drums:

Tama Superstar in Rosewood finish, with the inside of shells vibra-fibed (except timpani)

1. 14x24 bass drum
2. 5.5x14 "Old Faithful" Slingerland Artist snare drum
3. 5.5x6 concert tom
4. 5.5x8 concert tom
5. 6.5x10 concert tom
6. 8x12 concert tom
7. 8x12 tom
8. 9x13 tom
9. 12x15 tom
10. 16x18 floor tom
11. timpani
12. 6.5x13 Slingerland brass timbale
13. 6.5x14 Slingerland brass timbale

Cymbals:

Zildjian (except Wuhan)

A. 13" New Beat Hi-Hats
B. 20" Medium Crash
C. 16" Medium Crash
D. 8" Splash
E. 16" Medium Crash
F. 6" Splash
G. 22" Ping Ride
H. 18" Medium Crash
I. 20" Swish
J. 18" Wuhan Chinese
K. 18" Pang

Percussion:

aa. orchestra bells (glockenspiel)
bb. bell tree
cc. wind chimes (bar chimes)
dd. triangles
ee. cowbells
ff. Burma bell
gg. temple blocks
hh. large chimes
ii. gong
jj. chimes (tubular bells)
kk. crotales

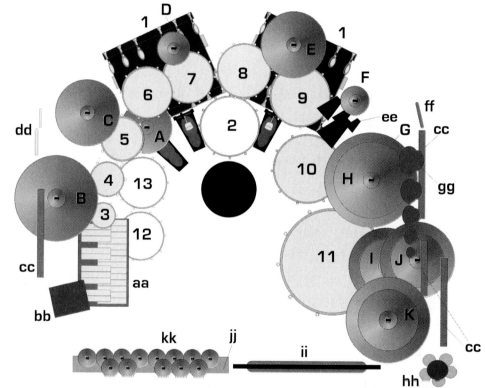

THE SPIRIT OF RADIO

Permanent Waves is considered one of Rush's seminal albums and a hard rock classic. Released in 1980, it marked a departure from the art-rock leanings of *A Farewell to Kings* and *Hemispheres*, while integrating a more concise songwriting style along with new stylistic elements. It can be said that this was the first album in which Rush truly crystallized its own brand of rock music. The album seems to beloved by just about all Rush fans, probably because it contains elements from the past and future of Rush. There are energetic, radio-friendly songs such as "The Spirit of Radio," "Free Will," and "Entre Nous," and yet the album also contains two longer tracks, "Natural Science" and "Jacob's Ladder," that are lingering favorites of progressive rock diehards.

Originally recorded for *Permanent Waves*, "The Spirit of Radio" was the opening song on the Time Machine tour, and hence also the first to appear on the *Taking Center Stage* DVD. This iconic song has been used as an opener by Rush on many tours, notably the *Moving Pictures* tour, where it was immortalized in fans' minds as the opening track on the multi-platinum live concert album and video, *Exit... Stage Left* (1981). The song's high energy, complex and aggressive opening riffs, great melodies, and upbeat message make it the perfect concert opener.

According to Neil, the song came together quickly, along with "Free Will" and "Jacob's Ladder," in the early writing stages for *Permanent Waves*. In those days, the band rehearsed the parts of each song many times over, and even performed the new material on tour before recording it, which explains the uncanny tightness with which the band plays the introductory riffs of this song.

ANALYSIS:

The most difficult section of the song is the introduction, which is reprised after the guitar solo. This section could have been written out many different ways, but I decided here to write it out without any dropped beats. Geddy, Alex, and Neil have been playing together for so long that they seem to have a unique way of interpreting certain rhythms, where they bend the time and feel things ahead or behind the beat together (as an unrelated example, think of the way a Latin percussionist stretches straight 16th-note rhythms into a unique type of swing). Because of this, not every note of the introductory riffs might fall in metronomic time according to the transcription, but I feel this is an accurate indication of what was played. Notice the orchestration of the various toms Neil uses. He begins with the higher register, and then uses larger toms once the guitar begins playing the unison figures along with the bass and drums.

In the pre-verse intro, we hear one of the earliest appearances of Neil's signature ride pattern (the first usage of this pattern appears on "La Villa Strangiato" from Rush's previous album, *Hemispheres*). This groove has become Neil's signature beat, identified so exclusively with him that no other drummer has recorded this exact pattern as Neil plays it. As explained on the *Taking Center Stage* DVD, the sticking is based on a right-hand paradiddle.

During the verse, the busy bass-drum pattern and well-placed hi-hat openings contribute to the forward motion of the groove. The chorus contains a bell melody that Neil originally played on orchestra bells, but is now played using bell samples on the MalletKAT. Leading out of the chorus is an interesting pattern where Neil's right hand alternates between his floor tom and crash cymbal. The coordination for this groove can take awhile to master.

The instrumental section in the middle of the song contains several measures of 7/4 time. This section should essentially be thought of as an eight-bar phrase, with one measure of 7/4 replacing every two bars of 4/4. When thought of this way, the phrasing makes sense: Three measures of 7/4, followed by two measures of 4/4. Also look out for the incorporation of the China cymbal on the upbeats as the energy builds, and the cool 32nd note-based fill leading into the solo section. Near the end of the song is an interesting reggae-inspired section with some creative cross-stick work. The influence of reggae would reappear on several subsequent Rush songs.

THE SPIRIT OF RADIO

THE SPIRIT OF RADIO

THE SPIRIT OF RADIO

THE SPIRIT OF RADIO

FREE WILL

"**F**ree Will" is another Rush classic from the album *Permanent Waves* (1980). On the *Taking Center Stage* DVD, Neil confirms that it is one of the most technically challenging Rush songs to play. The song is a perfect example of how the band's early experimentation with odd time signatures led to a mastery of them which could then be applied in the service of songwriting (and not just for technical display). Comparatively little of "Free Will" is in 4/4, yet the song flows wonderfully well, with the melody and vocal phrasing dictating the odd meters, similar to the song "Money" by Pink Floyd, but with more metric shifts. Even if using a transcription, it is possible (and probably preferable) to learn the song with no counting, just by following the melody.

The construction of the drum part in "Free Will" is masterful. Neil assigns each section of the piece a specific beat, and the band plays unison fill figures that build in complexity throughout the song. The guitar solo in this tune is one of the highlights of a live Rush show, and certainly among the most dense and chops-oriented of Neil's drum parts. The song also features some challenging polyrhythmic fills.

ANALYSIS:

After the two-bar descending intro (with cymbal chokes), the main melody of the song is stated, which consists of a bar of 6/4 and a bar of 7/4. All of the "pre-verse" sections follow this form (e.g. measures 5-8). The verses follow it as well, but modify it slightly by adding an extra beat at the end of the phrase (e.g. measures 10, 15). For this reason, I chose to transcribe the verses with long measures of 8/4 rather than two bars of 4/4, since these long measures really follow the 7/4 melody but with an added beat.

Measures 16-25 contain the pre-chorus, which is played in half-time (as compared to the verses and choruses); there is one backbeat in each bar. The first and second endings of each of these pre-choruses are orchestrated ensemble rhythms played by the entire band. These unison figures get more syncopated and challenging as the song progresses, building energy and excitement each time this section comes up.

The choruses of the song are built around a four-bar phrase of three bars of 4/4 time followed by one bar of 3/4. In each chorus, the end of the second phrase is punctuated by a signature drum fill (measures 33, 73, and 157-8). Also watch for punctuation of the end of the 3/4 phrase on the China cymbal.

Measure 55 contains an extremely challenging and exciting drum fill that blurs the location of the downbeat by using an accent pattern that essentially superimposes a feeling of "three" over the sixteenth-note pulse for four beats before rejoining the band for the unison accents leading into the pre-chorus. This is one of Neil's toughest fills to master.

The descending fill in measure 85 leads into the 6/8 guitar solo. The eighth note stays pretty much constant in the shift from 4/4 to 6/8, although in live performance the band usually picks up the tempo for this solo, and then pulls it back again after the solo is over. There are a ton of ghost notes on the snare drum throughout the solo, but they fall in very natural places, so focus first on the correct bass drum and snare accent placement, and then drop in the ghost notes. There are challenging figures throughout the solo, and just about all of these are also played by Geddy on the bass, making them essential to catch. Watch out especially at measures 120-121; this figure is very syncopated and should be counted out at first. From measures 113-135, when Neil is playing the ride cymbal, his left foot plays broken patterns on the hi-hat. These left-foot patterns are what feels comfortable for Neil, and can be left out until you feel comfortable with the rest of the groove. You could also play the left foot on the hi-hat on other beats if that works for you.

Take your time when learning this one. It's a beast!

FREE WILL

FREE WILL

FREE WILL

FREE WILL

FREE WILL

Natural Science

A n enduring prog-rock classic and fan favorite, "Natural Science" is the third song from the *Permanent Waves* album included in this book. On the *Taking Center Stage* DVD, it appears in the bonus features. It was not performed on the Time Machine tour, but instead was filmed on the previous *Snakes & Arrows* tour, and was included because of its wonderfully challenging drum part.

"Natural Science" and "Jacob's Ladder" are two long cuts on *Permanent Waves* that, to some fans, marked the end of Rush's purely progressive period, which most listeners equate with the epic-length songs on the albums *Caress of Steel*, *2112*, *A Farewell to Kings*, and *Hemispheres*. As Rush morphed into a more accessible, streamlined, and mature musical unit, these long songs and their progressive dressing gave way to the modern sound of the band. But for whatever reason, many Rush fans display a lingering fondness for these two particular songs. Rush relearned "Jacob's Ladder" for the Time Machine tour (it had not been played live since 1980), but felt that the song was too dated, so it was dropped.

As you look through this drum part, you will notice that "Natural Science" weaves in and out of several time signatures, but for the most part they can all be related back to the original quarter-note pulse of the song. Pay close attention to the pulse expressions given above the meter changes as you analyze the part.

This live version of the song is a slightly shorter arrangement than the original version on *Permanent Waves*.

ANALYSIS:

There is an extended guitar and vocal intro to the song which does not appear on the *Taking Center Stage* DVD, because there were no cameras pointing at Geddy or Alex. The chart picks up at the same place as the DVD, in the four-bar guitar pickup into the one-handed 16th-note opening groove. Notice the interesting left-foot hi-hat placement when Neil moves to the ride.

At measure 21, the song essentially shifts into double-time, and into a signature 7/8 melody which Neil ornaments in various ways through his groove variations. You will notice that 7/8 is occasionally broken by a measure of straight eighth notes in 2/4. Watch out for the little details like the snare/hi-hat fill in measure 35, and the various hi-hat openings throughout this part.

After the song switches to 4/4 (measures 50-65) and then back into 7, Neil punches the accents in the 7/8 melody on the China cymbal with quick double bass-drum triplets in between. When he returns to groove (bar 70), he is now playing with two hands on the hi-hat. The fill at measure 73 was originally played on a timbale, but here is placed on the 12" tom (Neil's 8", 10", and 12" toms are tuned quite high). As he loves to do, Neil continues to develop the part and introduce new ideas, moving to a bilateral ride/hi-hat riding pattern at measure 84.

Neil always handles the opportunity to play a drum break with incredible creativity. The two-bar break at measures 93-94 is no exception, with a cool little triplet pickup leading to some offbeat hi-hat barks, followed by descending triplets. Although the fill is challenging and somewhat busy, notice that Neil does not fill up every second of available space, but chooses to use variety in his rhythms to add an interesting tension that gets resolved when the band breaks into the next groove. Interestingly, the structure of this drum break is somewhat similar to the last of the signature drum breaks in "YYZ," which appeared on Rush's next album, *Moving Pictures*.

The arrangement of the song is quite challenging, as evidenced by all the different parts and shifts in feel. At measure 119, it switches to an interesting 12/8-2/4 pattern. This pattern could have been written out using 4/4 time for the entire pattern, but I chose to write it this way because it keeps the eighth-note pulse constant from the previous section. It is always easier to understand a song when you can relate the basic pulse of the sections to each other, even if the meter shifts. There are some fairly complex fills and patterns in measures 135-141, leading up to a release and change of tempo at measure 142.

From this point on, the song essentially shifts between a straight 4/4 groove, with the snare on all four downbeats, and a triplet 12/8 feel, with lots of Neil's signature details thrown in. There are interesting fills connecting all of these various subsections together. A really cool one appears in measure 175.

Natural Science

Neil shifts into a two-handed 12/8 pattern at measure 194, which entails his left hand coming down off the hi-hat to play the backbeat. Be careful with this groove because it is easy to get your hands tied up and/or get a poor-quality snare sound when coming down with the left hand. This section leads to the climax of the song, which comes complete with two long drum fills descending down the full array of toms on Neil's kit. The first one (measures 203-204) uses the flam accent rudiment, and the second (measures 205-206) is just a blazing barrage of singles.

"Natural Science" is chock-full of interesting grooves and fills, and packed with the spirit of Neil's creativity. Enjoy!

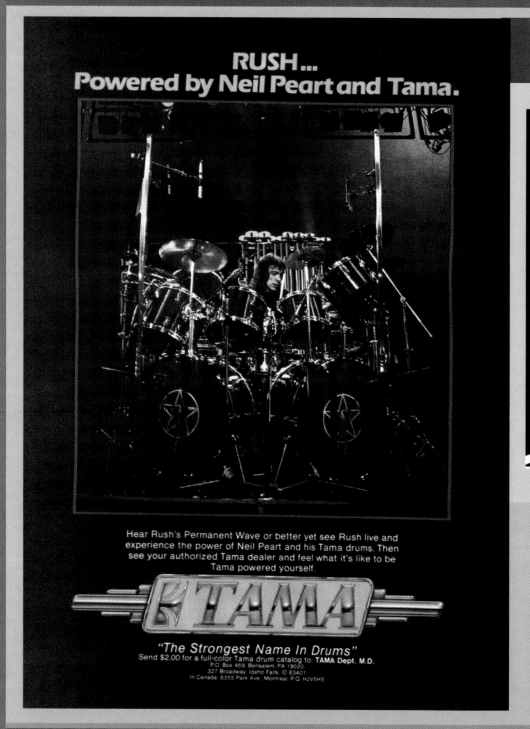

NATURAL SCIENCE

NATURAL SCIENCE

NATURAL SCIENCE

NATURAL SCIENCE

NATURAL SCIENCE

NATURAL SCIENCE

CHAPTER 5

For this tour, the one that saw Rush rise to bona fide rock superstardom, Neil kept the same rosewood-finished Tama Superstar kit he used on the *Permanent Waves* album and tour. These were amazing-sounding drums, and the drum sound on the *Moving Pictures* album was considered one of the best ever recorded up until that time. Rush also had developed a reputation for having great concert sound (as well as being excellent players). Of course, great sound always starts with the player and the instrument, and Neil embraced a timeless and resonant drum sound, rather than the "dead" sound many players used in the late 1970s and early 1980s.

There were a couple of fairly significant changes in the drum setup for the *Moving Pictures* tour, however. The most significant was the retiring of the timpani and gong, and their replacement with two Tama gong bass drums. These were developed by Tama with Billy Cobham, and were soon adapted by Simon Phillips (the drummer perhaps best known for his use of this particular instrument). It is interesting that Neil used two of them at first; their timbre and pitch were likely quite similar. This is probably why, after one more tour, he got rid of one of them. The gong bass drum stayed in his setup until his switch to DW drums, being refinished and retrofitted for each new kit (at that time, there were no other manufacturers who made a gong drum). The only other change to the actual drums on the kit was the replacement of the old timbales with new wood-shell Tama Superstar ones.

Looking at Neil's tour book notes, one interesting thing to note is his choice of Evans Hydraulic drumheads for the bottoms of his closed tom-toms. These heads are extremely dead, consisting of two plys of plastic film with oil sandwiched in between. Perhaps their lack of resonance made a more uniform sound between the concert toms and the closed toms. Whatever the reason, these heads have never been a common choice for use as resonant/bottom heads.

The setup diagrammed here can be heard on the *Exit… Stage Left* album and concert video. The beginning of that concert film contains a few brief clips of Neil's kit being set up for a show while "The Camera Eye" plays in the background. Studious fans will notice that the *Taking Center Stage* DVD uses the same song (albeit the Time Machine tour 2011 version) as the backing music to its drum setup segment—a little homage to the classic *Exit... Stage Left* video!

From the Moving Pictures tour book, Neil writes:

I am still releasing my hostilities on Tama drums, all with wooden shells, and the inner side "vibra-fibed." The bass drums are 24", the toms are 6", 8", 10", 12" concerts, and 12", 13", 15", and 18" closed toms. I am still using my "Old Faithful" wood-shell snare, a 5-1/2" x 14" Slingerland, and have recently made a switch to wooden timbales, and retired my tympani and gong in favor of a pair of Tama gong bass drums, which are open-ended bass drums on a stand, utilizing oversize heads to give a very deep, resonant sound. My cymbals are Avedis Zildjians, with the exception of one genuine Chinese China type. The Zildjians are 8" and 10" splash, 13" hi-hats, two 16" and one each 18" and 20" crash cymbals, a 22" ride, an 18" pang, and a 20" China type. In the Percussion Department are orchestra bells, tubular bells, wind chimes, temple blocks, cowbells, triangles, bell tree, crotales, and Burma bell. I use Remo Clear Dots on my snare and bass drums, Ludwig Silver Dots on the concert toms, and Evans Looking Glass (top), and blue Hydraulic (bottom) on the closed toms. Clear Remos are used on the timbales and gong bass drums. Ludwig pedals, Slingerland hi-hat, Tama hardware, and Pro-Mark 747 drumsticks are the final details.

DRUM SETUP

Drums:

Tama Superstar in Rosewood finish,
with the inside of shells vibra-fibed

1. 14x24 bass drum
2. 5.5x14 "Old Faithful" Slingerland
   Artist snare drum
3. 5.5x6 concert tom
4. 5.5x8 concert tom
5. 6.5x10 concert tom
6. 8x12 concert tom
7. 8x12 tom
8. 9x13 tom
9. 12x15 tom
10. 16x18 floor tom
11. 14x22 gong bass drum
12. 14x20 gong bass drum
13. 6.5x13 Tama wood timbale
14. 6.5x14 Tama wood timbale

Cymbals:

Zildjian (except Wuhan)

A. 13" New Beat Hi-Hats
B. 20" Medium Thin Crash
C. 16" Medium Thin Crash
D. 10" Splash
E. 16" Medium Thin Crash
F. 8" Splash
G. 22" Ping Ride
H. 18" Medium Thin Crash
I. 20" Swish
J. 18" Wuhan Chinese
K. 18" Pang

Percussion:

aa. orchestra bells
   (glockenspiel)
bb. bell tree
cc. wind chimes (bar chimes)
dd. triangles
ee. cowbells
ff. Burma bell
gg. temple blocks
hh. large chimes
ii. chimes (tubular bells)
jj. crotales

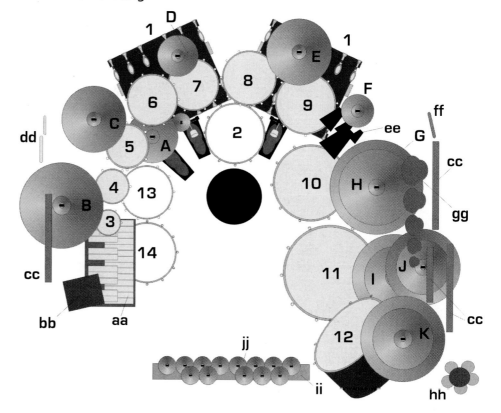

Tom Sawyer

Probably the best-known Rush song, "Tom Sawyer" was a hit single on the Billboard charts in both the United States and the UK. It is the opening song on *Moving Pictures* (1981), an all-time classic among rock albums, which itself rose to number 3 on the Billboard charts in the United States, and was certified quadruple platinum in 1995. After the success of *Permanent Waves*, Rush planned to continue touring and release another live album, but according to Neil (in the *Moving Pictures* tour book), after a show at the Palladium in New York City on May 9, 1980, the band decided that they were hitting a creative peak, and returned to the studio instead.

Rush's instincts turned out to be right in a big way. The new directions that began with "The Spirit of Radio," "Entre Nous," and "Free Will" crystallized into a set of new material that truly cemented the band's original approach, moving them away from the progressive rock niche and into the realm of full-blown rock stardom. At this point, the songwriting and arranging had become incredibly strong, and was now concentrated into a much more accessible package of shorter, well constructed songs (although *Moving Pictures* does contain one epic song, "The Camera Eye," which clocks in at 11 minutes).

Rush fans were thrilled when the band announced that it would perform the *Moving Pictures* album in its entirety on the Time Machine tour. Although the band has regularly performed all of the songs from side one of the album, "Witch Hunt" was somewhat more rare, and "The Camera Eye" had not been performed since the *Signals* tour in 1982.

A note about the choice of transcriptions: All of the drum parts on *Moving Pictures* are classics, but due to the fact that most of them have been transcribed in various other books, I decided here to include the two songs most popular with drummers, "Tom Sawyer" and "YYZ." If you would like to study a transcription of the original recording of "The Camera Eye," that song is included in another of my books, *MD Classic Tracks* (Modern Drummer Publications).

ANALYSIS:

Neil is often asked if he ever gets bored playing "Tom Sawyer," because it is always included in the setlist. His response is always the same: The song is so difficult to play that it could never become boring. In addition to the challenges presented by the odd-meter sections and complex grooves and fills, a huge part of the difficulty is the endurance required to maintain the driving sixteenth-note pulse of the song with one hand. For this reason, Neil prefers the song to appear later in the setlist, although the band opened with it on the *Vapor Trails* tour (2002).

The opening sections of the song, from the introduction through the first verse and bridge, are fairly easy to understand, but difficult to execute with Neil's precision and power. After the ensemble figures at measure 13, check out the busy bass-drum pattern underneath the ride cymbal work in measures 14-16. The loose hi-hat eighth notes in bars 26-30 give the right hand a slight break before launching back into the next verse. One look at all of the people air-drumming this part at a Rush concert will tell you that the grooves in the verses of the song (more specifically, the placement of the bass drum part and hi-hat openings) fit so well that the listener expects to hear them just as written.

The keyboard solo section begins at measure 35, with the song switching into 7/8 time, and the groove incorporating a two-bar phrase with carefully placed hi-hat openings. After a creative fill in measure 44, Neil switches to the ride and begins to change the placement of the snare accents, which builds the excitement and tension of this part. The first and second endings (bars 48-51) present an interesting turnaround with a couple of very odd measures (which Neil said originated in a mistake while he was learning the song!). From there, Neil continues to build tension by increasing the density of snare notes, incorporating the China, and eventually going to quarter notes on the snare as he builds into the ensemble figures before his big fills.

The featured drum fills (bars 59-62) are masterfully designed, using many of the voices on Neil's large kit, and deftly incorporating the band figures into the drum part. The fast 32nd notes down the toms in measure 59 are interrupted by a crash cymbal; notice how the inclusion of this voice in the middle of a tom-tom run drives the excitement up another level. The clean and precise tom-tom/bass drum "quads" in measure 60 have been copied by every drummer who has ever heard this song, and the following two measures incorporate exciting and creative syncopation between the toms and crash cymbals. There's a whole lot of drumming ingenuity jammed into these four bars!

After the drum breaks, the sixteenth-note groove returns, but this time with greater intensity. There are snare hits on every beat, eventually building to quick 32nd notes in measure 67, surrounding the band accents. Following this, measures 68-70 push your endurance even further with busy, quick ghost notes between the accents, and then another fast 32nd-note fill at measure 71. It's probably best to make sure you are warmed up before attempting this song!

After the final verse/chorus, the song shifts back to 7/8 and incorporates the same 7/16-3/8 turnaround as the keyboard and guitar solos, but with different syncopations in the groove and different fills that are (as is always the case with Neil) perfectly orchestrated to fit with the song. The one at measure 93 is especially interesting because of where it starts in the measure and the incorporation of the flam on the last beat.

TOM SAWYER

TOM SAWYER

TOM SAWYER

TOM SAWYER

YYZ

"YYZ" is one of the best-known rock instrumentals of all time. The song was nominated for a Grammy as Best Rock Instrumental in 1982, and its drum part was studied with awe by an entire generation of drummers that grew up in the 1980s. Bands that have covered the song include Primus, Phish, Dream Theater, Godsmack, Umphrey's McGee, and Muse. From its release on *Moving Pictures* in 1981, it has remained a staple of Rush's live concerts, performed on every tour since then. The rhythmic motif at the beginning of the song is the Morse code for the letters "Y-Y-Z." Neil came up with the idea of using this rhythm as the basis for a song as he was sitting in the cockpit of a small airplane flying into Toronto's Pearson International Airport (call letters YYZ), and heard the Morse code being sent out by the beacon there. This rhythm is in 5/4 time, and Neil originally played it on a single crotale to introduce the song, but now uses two differently pitched crotale samples triggered from pads.

After the Morse code 5/4 intro, "YYZ" settles into a driving rock groove with funk inflections, and contains a set of amazing drum and bass guitar breaks that have kept musicians in the practice room for hours. Pay special attention to how tight the ensemble of Alex, Geddy, and Neil sounds. They are completely locked in, from the challenging rhythmic intro, to the uncanny tightness of the unison riffs that follow it, to the slick grooves of the main sections of the song. One thing you'll notice if you attempt to play along to the song is that Neil tends to make his parts look easier than they are. "YYZ" goes by at a very brisk tempo, especially for some of the intricate drum parts that Neil has devised for the song. It is very easy to tense up during these busier sections. If you are learning a drum part like this, it is always best to start slow and make sure that you can work things up to tempo with your muscles relaxed; otherwise your grooves and fills will sound very stiff. As Neil found with Freddie Gruber, working with a professional drum teacher is often the best way to fine-tune your skills, in order to make sure you are approaching the instrument with the best possible technique.

ANALYSIS:

The 5/4 theme is stated with snare drum and hi-hat in the first four measures after the intro, after which Neil switches to the ride. The ride cymbal maintains straight eighth notes while the bass drum follows the theme, which can present some coordination challenges at first, especially given how the left-foot hi-hat interacts with the rest of the groove. It is important to keep your hands relaxed during the quick 32nd-note fills that connect the intro together.

The unison figures in measures 14-16 are played with extreme tightness and precision by the band. After the initial two-beat rest in bar 13, the time feels somewhat elastic, but after playing together for thirty years, Geddy, Alex, and Neil obviously know how to feel this the exact same way. On the DVD, Neil and I discussed how initially the band looked at each other when playing this section, but I have noticed at Rush concerts over the years that they no longer need to do so.

YYZ

After the meaty quarter-note "verse" (bars 17-32), a tasty snare flam/tom-run fill leads into Neil's signature ride pattern, which fits perfectly here. The three endings of this section (bars 37, 38, 39) each feature a drum fill that is challenging to execute at this tempo. The first ending contains two quick left-hand hi-hat barks, the second ending drops in a couple of quick double bass-drum 32nd notes leading up to a flam on the snare and a quick China-cymbal accent, and the third integrates flams alternating with bass-drum strokes. These fills pass by very quickly at this tempo, and require the hands and feet to be relaxed for clean execution. After the third ending comes the bridge section featuring the bass and drum breaks; this section uses an interesting groove featuring open offbeats on the hi-hat and several well-placed ghost notes.

The drum breaks themselves each have their own personality, and are quite musical and memorable. The first one (measure 47) uses a 32nd note-based rhythm around the drums that Neil credits as being inspired by Terry Bozzio (whom he saw perform with Frank Zappa), while Bozzio credits the great Tony Williams as the originator of this type of lick. The second break (bar 55) uses sixteenth-note triplets leading into an interesting orchestration of a few sixteenth notes that ends with an offbeat crash. The final break (measures 64-65) is twice as long as the others, and contains another syncopated accent pattern and a long, descending tom run. On *Moving Pictures* Neil was still using concert toms as the highest voices on his kit, while on his current setup all of the toms are double-headed. It is always interesting to hear how Neil executes some of his classic drum parts on his evolving setup.

There is a guitar solo beginning at measure 66, which is accompanied once again by Neil's signature ride pattern, except this time there are China cymbal accents with double bass that punctuate the end of the phrases. Notice how Neil integrates the "broken glass" sample sound into these figures. If you look at measures 69, 73, and 77, you will notice that the sample is not played in the same place in any of those measures. After another stop-time break at measure 81, there is a half-time keyboard interlude which Neil punctuates with well-placed crash accents and a few tasteful fills using the toms. This section leads back into the main "verse" theme, and Neil uses one of his favorite musical devices: playing a fill in the same place, but expanding the fill each time that place comes up. A great example of this happens in measures 107-108, where Neil stretches his fill out to last for two full measures. The same principle is applied in measure 115: The run down the toms now begins with a quick flurry of 32nd notes, where in the first verse, it was simply sixteenth notes.

After a nimble double bass-drum fill in measure 130, the song ends with a long descending band figure that echoes Neil's first drum break, followed by a one-measure reprise of the Morse code theme and a descending triplet that punctuates the end of the song. All in all, "YYZ" contains most of the elements that have made Neil such a legendary and popular drummer: creative musical themes, well-orchestrated signature fills, energetic rock grooves, and all-around exciting playing. And let's not forget another important reason why drummers love to play this song: It's *fun*.

YYZ

YYZ

Glass breaking sample

YYZ

YYZ

CHAPTER 6

SIGNALS TOUR
(1982-83)

During the mixing of *Exit… Stage Left*, Neil had a bit of downtime, and just for fun he acquired and restored an old set of Hayman drums. He enjoyed how open and resonant this small kit sounded, and felt that he wanted a little more of that type of sound from his regular Rush drumset. So he approached Tama about making him a new set with thinner shells (which would resonate more freely). Neil had achieved a state-of-the-art sound on *Moving Pictures*, and he was among the vanguard of top drummers at the time who were quickly trending away from the dead, duct-taped, concert tom sound of the 1970s. Drum manufacturers were beginning to take notice.

Tama rose to the occasion. After using the first Superstar kit for two albums and long tours, Neil retired those drums and got a new set, this time in a custom Candy Apple Red finish, which would stay with him for the next three albums and tours. Neil was at an extreme pinnacle in popularity amongst drummers at this time, so he and his drums were featured extensively in Tama and Zildjian advertisements. In fact, among Rush and Neil fans, one of the most sought-after collectible items is a silkscreen banner that Tama manufactured and distributed to its dealers to hang in their drum shops in the early 1980s. This banner featured Neil playing his new Tama kit on a raft in the middle of a lake, with green forest in the background. These were truly "dream drums" for many a young drummer!

Tama called this drumset the prototype for their new Artstar line of drums, but they were actually far different. These drums were modified Superstars (like Neil's last kit)—they were made from the same wood (birch) and had the exact same hoops and lug casings. The main difference was that the shells were thinner (four-ply, where the old ones were six-ply), and thus more resonant, which was what Neil was after. The actual Artstar drums that Tama released in 1983 were also birch shells, but with an interior and exterior ply of Cordia (and only offered in the natural Cordia finish), and they had hardware that was much different from the Superstars. In 1986 Tama released the Artstar II series, which were even more different, consisting of 7mm, nine-ply maple shells. In addition to trending towards thicker shells, many (if not most) of the Superstar and Artstar drums purchased by Neil fans in the early 1980s were ultra-deep power toms, which were all the rage at the time, but which have fallen completely out of fashion today. Neil's drums were (and still are) traditional "jazz"-sized drums, and, interestingly, traditional-sized Tama Superstar drums in good condition are quite sought-after on the vintage drum market today (although none have the same shells as Neil's custom Artstar prototype; they were unique).

Neil also switched at this time to using all Tama hardware, retiring his Ludwig Speed King pedals in favor of new Tama Camco ones, and adding a Tama Titan hi-hat stand. The sizes and configuration of the new kit matched the previous one exactly, including a new pair of Tama wood timbales and gong bass drums. As the music evolved, Neil also began to gradually scale down his percussion setup, getting rid of a few triangles and bells.

Neil was still using his well-traveled "Old Faithful" Slingerland snare drum at this time, which up until now was still sporting its original copper finish. Since the drum began to look "tacky" (Neil's words) with his new red kit, he took a bit of a chance and had it disassembled and refinished to match the rest of the set. Apparently this had no negative effects on its sound, because he continued to use this very same snare drum for another decade, and had it refinished many more times.

From the Signals tour book, Neil writes:

Well, well! Hello again for another tour! (This is getting to be habit forming!) I've got some new drums to tell you about. Once again, they are Tamas; with the custom candy apple red finish, the brass plated hardware, and the vibra-fibing of the inner shells performed by The Percussion Center of Fort Wayne. The sizes remain the same: two 24" bass drums, 6", 8", 10", and 12" concert toms, 12", 13", 15", and 18" closed toms, and 20" and 22" gong bass drums. My snare is still the same old wood-shell Slingerland, and I am using the Tama wooden timbales with great satisfaction. With the exception of the trashy Chinese cymbal, all my cymbals are by Avedis Zildjian. They are: 8" and 10" splash, 13" hi-hats, two 16" crashes, one each 18" and 20" crash, a 22" ride, an 18" pang, and a 20" China type. In the Department of Percussion Effects are orchestra bells, tubular bells, wind chimes, temple blocks, numerous semi-melodic cowbells, triangle, bell tree, and crotales. There are Remo Clear Dot heads on the snare and bass drums, Evans Heavy Duty Rock on all the toms and the gong bass drums, and Evans Tom-Tom models on the bottoms of the closed toms. These are all non-Hydraulic heads. I use clear Remos on the timbales. All of the stands and hardware are by Tama, and I am still using Pro-Mark 747 sticks, with the varnish removed from the gripping area by Larry.

And that's all!

DRUM SETUP

Drums:

Tama Artstar prototype in Candy Apple Red finish, with the inside of shells vibra-fibed

1. 14x24 bass drum
2. 5.5x14 "Old Faithful" Slingerland Artist snare drum
3. 5.5x6 concert tom
4. 5.5x8 concert tom
5. 6.5x10 concert tom
6. 8x12 concert tom
7. 8x12 tom
8. 9x13 tom
9. 12x15 tom
10. 16x18 floor tom
11. 14x22 gong bass drum
12. 14x20 gong bass drum
13. 6.5x13 Tama wood timbale
14. 6.5x14 Tama wood timbale

Cymbals:

Zildjian (except Wuhan)

A. 13" New Beat Hi-Hats
B. 20" Medium Thin Crash
C. 16" Medium Thin Crash
D. 10" Splash
E. 16" Medium Thin Crash
F. 8" Splash
G. 22" Ping Ride
H. 18" Medium Thin Crash
I. 20" Swish
J. 18" Wuhan Chinese
K. 18" Pang

Percussion:

aa. orchestra bells (glockenspiel)
bb. bell tree
cc. wind chimes (bar chimes)
dd. triangle
ee. cowbells
ff. temple blocks
gg. large chimes
hh. chimes (tubular bells)
ii. crotales

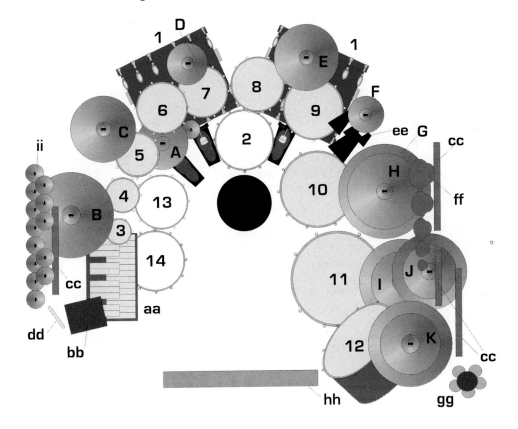

SUBDIVISIONS

The *Signals* album was represented on the Time Machine tour by "Subdivisions," another all-time Rush classic and fan favorite. Released in 1982 and following the huge success of *Moving Pictures*, *Signals* was somewhat controversial among Rush fans at the time because of the way the band's style was developing. *Signals*, like much of the music of the early 1980s, used keyboards and synthesizers at the forefront of its sound. Although some fans of the harder-edged styles of previous albums were upset by this development, in retrospect it is clear that Rush's constant push to change, develop, and incorporate new sounds is one of the key ingredients to their long-term success.

"Subdivisions," as a drum part, is one of Neil's true masterpieces. The song is jam-packed with creative ideas that are carefully orchestrated into a drum part that becomes one with the song. All the elements that have made Neil one of the most influential drummers in history are present here: creative and unique grooves, cool fills, deft handling of odd meters, carefully crafted and orchestrated parts using the entire large kit, and challenging technical elements.

ANALYSIS:

By this time in their development, the use of odd time signatures had become typical of Rush, and "Subdivisions"

uses odd meters without really drawing a lot of attention to them. The song switches between 4/4, 7/8, and 6/4 in a seamless fashion, due to both the writing of the song itself, and the way Neil's drum part smoothly ties it all together. The song starts in 7/8, and Neil's entrance stays in 7 until measure 9, where the time shifts to 4/4. Notice how Neil uses the splash cymbal to accent the last two beats of the second ending (bar 7). His orchestration of the splash and China cymbals in this song demonstrates how he has mastered orchestrating the cymbal voices to fit the song. These sound choices are always carefully considered.

At measure 13 Neils shifts to a two-surface ride/hi-hat pattern with a half-time feel and some syncopated snare accents dropped in. Notice how all the downbeats except for beat 3 are de-emphasized in this groove. This leads to two signature fills in the two endings (measures 18, 19), and another example (of many in this tune) of great cymbal orchestration: the use of the China cymbal to follow the band figures in measures 20-22.

The first verse starts with a straight rock groove (bars 24-27) before shifting back into 7/8 at measure 28. The 7/8 groove is anchored by a left-hand diddle on the snare drum leading into open hi-hat on beat 1 of the bar. After reprising the band figure from bar 21, but using the hi-hat instead of China this time, the intro theme is returned to again, and during these sections (bars 37-41), the snare drum backbeats are dropped out except for key accents. The song shifts back to 7/8 again at bar 41, and Neil modifies the 7/8 groove by placing an alternating pattern at the end of the bar (this type of hi-hat "bark" pattern was often used by Phil Collins, who was an influence on Neil).

The chorus of "Subdivisions" is anchored by a straight rock groove played on loose hi-hats, but as is usually the case with Rush, there is an interesting twist in the addition of two beats at the end of the four-bar phrase, making a measure of 6/4. The bridge section after the chorus (measures 61-70) stays in 6/4, with Neil's signature ride pattern cleverly modified to fit this section.

A creative and tricky drum fill at bar 70 leads into the second intro, verse, and chorus of the song, and you'll notice that Neil is not content to simply repeat the parts from the first intro/verse, but invents new ways to articulate each of these sections.

After the keyboard and guitar solos, a wonderfully energetic fill at bar 126 leads into the ending section of the song. As the song builds to a climax, Neil introduces a right-hand cymbal ostinato with the ride cymbal on the downbeats and the China cymbal on the upbeats. He keeps this pattern going throughout the ending, placing various snare accents around it, and eventually goes to a driving quarter-note snare drum groove. This section masterfully raises the energy of the song to a climax, only to be driven even higher by the soloistic fills Neil plays around the band figures to bring the song to a close. In these fills, Neil's left foot moves to the double pedal, allowing him to drop in the two-foot patterns shown. This entire ending section is a technical challenge, yet musically fits in perfectly with the composition.

SUBDIVISIONS

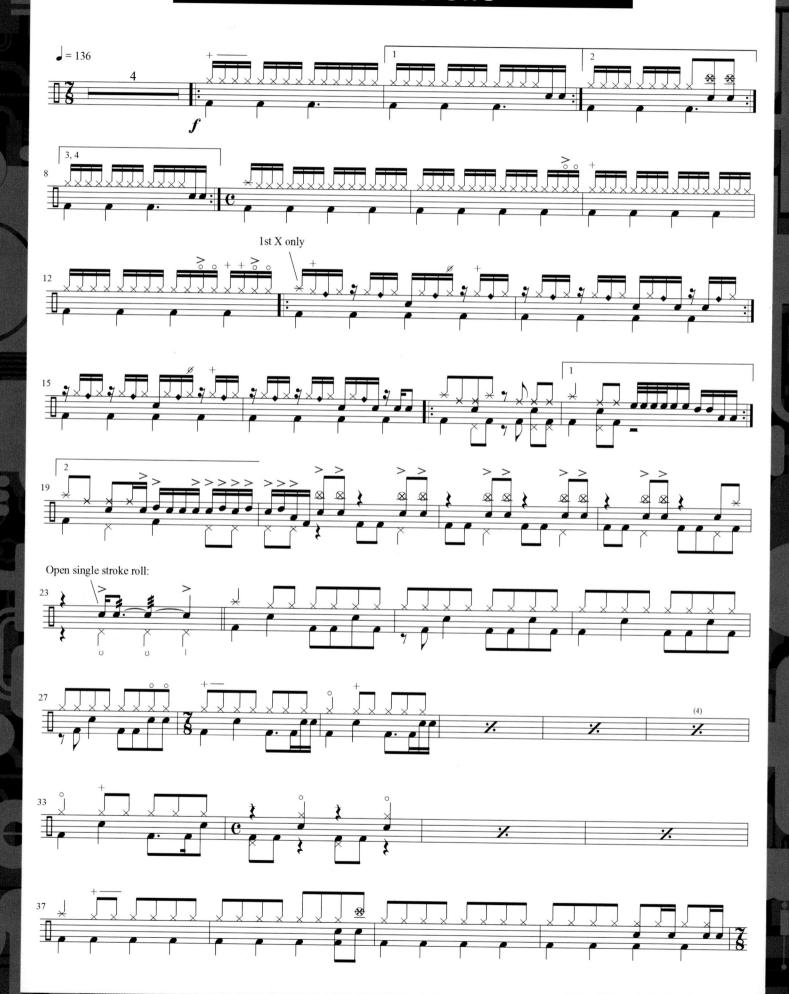

SUBDIVISIONS

SUBDIVISIONS

SUBDIVISIONS

CHAPTER 7

GRACE UNDER PRESSURE AND POWER WINDOWS TOURS

(1984-86)

Although for these two tours Neil kept the same Tama Artstar prototype drums he had used on the *Signals* album and tour, nevertheless he made some very significant and cool changes to his drum rig. For the *Grace Under Pressure* album, Neil began using electronic drums. These were made by Simmons, who were the leaders in this area at the time. Because Neil did not want to compromise or change his main drumset, he came up with the idea of having a separate, smaller electronic kit facing the opposite direction, which he could play by just turning around on the same drum throne. His first "rear kit" consisted of four Simmons pads, plus an acoustic snare drum (another Slingerland "Artist" model), bass drum (interestingly, a small 18"), and a small acoustic cymbal setup.

At this time, Rush would on occasion go out and play a few live shows before recording a new album, both to hone their playing chops before recording, and to "road test" some of the new songs. This they did in 1983 with a series of sold-out shows at Radio City Music Hall in New York City. Neil had devised and assembled his rear kit, and for these shows he turned around and played with his back to the audience! This being a strange position for any musician to be in, there was only one thing to do: build a rotating drum riser so that Neil could always face the front. And so it was done. Neil hit the road for 1984's *Grace Under Pressure* tour with his first octagonal rotating riser!

When Neil and his team made this riser, it was designed in such a way that it took the customization of Neil's kit to a whole new level. First, with the advent of the electronic setup, much of his acoustic percussion was retired. Having gotten rid of the timpani and gong a couple of years earlier, now the bell tree, tubular bells, and a few sets of bar chimes also disappeared. In order to house the remaining percussion instruments, symmetrical overhead bars were built on either side of the riser, and the bar chimes, temple blocks, and crotales were mounted from these (actually, there had been a similar set of bars going back as far as the *Permanent Waves/Moving Pictures* kit, but with a different instrument configuration). The second big customization was designing the riser so that it would accept specially designed threaded-pipe cymbal stands, thereby eliminating all the tripods on the cymbal and tom stands. This gave Neil's kit a unique, uncluttered, and sleek appearance. He still uses the same design concept with his current riser and setup, and nearly every aspect of the appearance of his drumset is custom: the finish on the drums, the finish on the stands and hardware, the design of the stands (to fit the riser), and the riser itself.

For the *Power Windows* tour, the drumset remained essentially the same, but a major leap forward was made in that Neil became deeply involved with sampling at this time. The electronic setup, based on the state-of-the-art Simmons SDS-7 brain with "Erasable Programmable Read-Only Memory (EPROM)," allowed Neil to reproduce live the dozens of custom percussion sounds he used on the *Power Windows* album. Neil, along with other great rock drummers like Bill Bruford, was a trailblazer in the area of electronic percussion and especially sampling in the 1980s.

Tama made a duplicate of this drumset for the Japanese dates on the *Grace Under Pressure* tour. Much later, they also made a Starclassic Maple version of it for Mike Portnoy for his Rush tribute band, Cygnus and the Sea Monsters. Neil gave away this drumset via a contest in *Modern Drummer*, and it eventually surfaced (of course) on eBay, where it was purchased and restored by Rush collector, fan, and author Robert Telleria.

The diagram on page 113 shows the *Power Windows* tour kit.

From the Grace Under Pressure tour book, Neil writes:

Hi there folks! I'm the blurry blob in the middle of all those DRUMS! I don't know where they come from, but every time I turn around there are more of them! When they're packed away in those dark, warm cases—you don't suppose they...? (Eerie music fades up)

"You are entering a world of imagination..."

You are entering a world of *drums*—that's what! I've got drums literally coming and going this year. Everywhere I turn, more of 'em, closing in around me. More and more of them, getting bigger and bigger—and they're red!! Red, like—*blood! "Izzen dat scaddy kids?"* O-O-W-H-O-O-O-o-o-o.

O-kay!... Ahem. The main kit remains the same, the prototype for what they're calling the Tama *Artstar* drums these days. Two 24" bass drums, 6", 8", 10", and 12" concert toms, 12", 13", 15", and 18" closed toms, and a 22" gong bass drum is the basic outfit. The "Old Faithful" 5.5x14" Slingerland snare is still number one, and I am again using a metal timbale, a 13" Tama to be exact.

The cymbals of course are by Avedis Zildjian, 8" and 10" splash, 13" hi-hats, two 16" crashes, one each 18" and 20" crash, a 22" ride (ten years old now!), an 18" pang, and a 20" China type. There is also a China type which is really from China (as opposed to America, Switzerland, Italy or Turkey). On the rear kit there are *more* Zildjians—another 22" ride, 16" and 18" crash, 13" hi-hats, and another of those Chinese jobs.

The rear set consists of a Tama 18" bass drum, another Slingerland snare, three Simmons tom modules and one snare module, and the Simmons "Clap Trap" with foot switches both fore and aft.

The incidental percussion department is also in a state of change as we speak, but may consist of orchestra bells, wind chimes, crotales, temple blocks, cowbells, and/or a bell tree. I'm just not sure.

I'm still using the Remo Clear Dot heads on the snare(s) and bass drums, Evans Heavy Duty Rock (top) and Evans Tom Tom (bottom) on the closed toms, Remo Black Dots on the concert toms, and plain clear Remos on the timbale and gong bass drums. All of the hardware (but for a couple of small bits) is by Tama, as are the Camco chain-drive pedals, and I'm still chewing up Pro-Mark 747 sticks, which have the varnish filed off the shoulder area by Larry. (He's the blurry blob in the back tearing his hair and gnashing his teeth over the drums, the monitors, the headphones, the electronics and all of the presets for the Simmons and the Clap Trap!)

AH-HA-HA-HA-ha-ha!! (O-o-o-o-o... scaddy!)

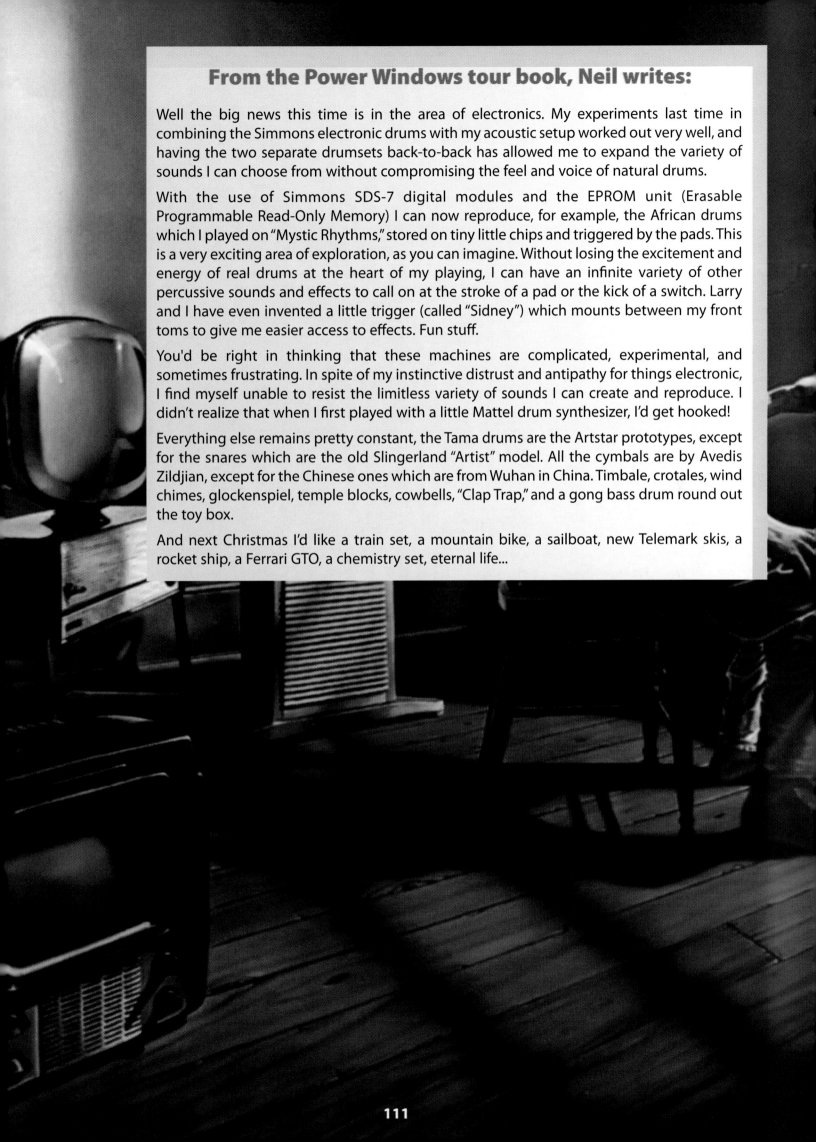

From the Power Windows tour book, Neil writes:

Well the big news this time is in the area of electronics. My experiments last time in combining the Simmons electronic drums with my acoustic setup worked out very well, and having the two separate drumsets back-to-back has allowed me to expand the variety of sounds I can choose from without compromising the feel and voice of natural drums.

With the use of Simmons SDS-7 digital modules and the EPROM unit (Erasable Programmable Read-Only Memory) I can now reproduce, for example, the African drums which I played on "Mystic Rhythms," stored on tiny little chips and triggered by the pads. This is a very exciting area of exploration, as you can imagine. Without losing the excitement and energy of real drums at the heart of my playing, I can have an infinite variety of other percussive sounds and effects to call on at the stroke of a pad or the kick of a switch. Larry and I have even invented a little trigger (called "Sidney") which mounts between my front toms to give me easier access to effects. Fun stuff.

You'd be right in thinking that these machines are complicated, experimental, and sometimes frustrating. In spite of my instinctive distrust and antipathy for things electronic, I find myself unable to resist the limitless variety of sounds I can create and reproduce. I didn't realize that when I first played with a little Mattel drum synthesizer, I'd get hooked!

Everything else remains pretty constant, the Tama drums are the Artstar prototypes, except for the snares which are the old Slingerland "Artist" model. All the cymbals are by Avedis Zildjian, except for the Chinese ones which are from Wuhan in China. Timbale, crotales, wind chimes, glockenspiel, temple blocks, cowbells, "Clap Trap," and a gong bass drum round out the toy box.

And next Christmas I'd like a train set, a mountain bike, a sailboat, new Telemark skis, a rocket ship, a Ferrari GTO, a chemistry set, eternal life...

DRUM SETUP

Drums:

Tama Artstar prototype in Candy Apple Red finish, with the inside of shells vibra-fibed

1. 14x24 bass drum
2. 5.5x14 "Old Faithful" Slingerland Artist snare drum
3. 5.5x6 concert tom
4. 5.5x8 concert tom
5. 6.5x10 concert tom
6. 8x12 concert tom
7. 8x12 tom
8. 9x13 tom
9. 12x15 tom
10. 16x18 floor tom
11. 14x22 gong bass drum
12. 6.5x13 Tama brass timbale
13. 5x14 Slingerland Artist snare drum
14. 14x18 bass drum

Cymbals:

Zildjian (except Wuhan)

A. 13" New Beat Hi-Hats
B. 20" Medium Thin Crash
C. 16" Medium Thin Crash
D. 10" Splash
E. 16" Medium Thin Crash
F. 8" Splash
G. 22" Ping Ride
H. 18" Medium Thin Crash
I. 20" Swish
J. 18" Wuhan Chinese
K. 18" Pang
L. 13" New Beat Hi-Hats
M. 18" Medium Thin Crash
N. 22" Ping Ride
O. 16" Medium Thin Crash
P. 20" Wuhan Chinese

Percussion & Electronics:

aa. orchestra bells (glockenspiel)
bb. crotales
cc. wind chimes (bar chimes)
dd. cowbells
ee. temple blocks
ff. Simmons SDS-7 tom module
gg. Simmons SDS-7 snare module

Additional Electronics:
Simmons Clap Trap with foot switches
Simmons SDS-7 brain with EPROM unit

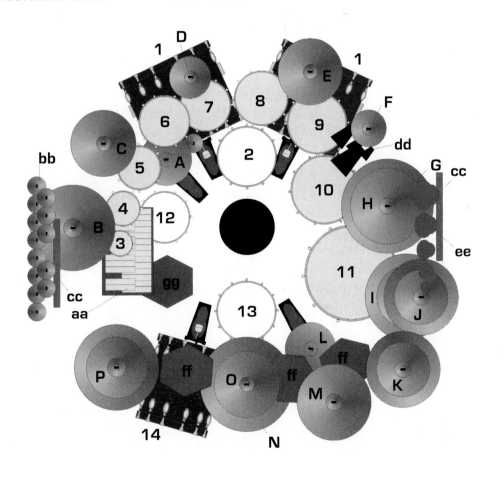

MARATHON

After 1982's *Signals*, which expanded the use of keyboards in Rush's sound, the band continued to push the technological envelope with *Grace Under Pressure* (1984) and *Power Windows* (1985). These two albums, the first to be completed without longtime co-producer Terry Brown, saw Neil delve deeply into the world of electronic percussion. On the *Grace Under Pressure* album and tour, Neil was using Simmons drums and, for the most part, employed on-board electronic sounds (for example, check out the song "Red Sector A"). By the time *Power Windows* rolled around, Neil had begun to incorporate sampling into his electronic setup. This widened his sound palette tremendously, since he could take almost any percussion instrument, sample it, and then trigger the sound from his electronic pads. As a result, *Power Windows* contains a dizzying array of different sounds (African drums, bongos, effects) which could be reproduced exactly in a concert setting via sampling. For drummers, *Power Windows* is one of Neil's richest, most creative, and most intelligent pieces of work. The incorporation of all the new sounds just added another level of artistry to Neil's rhythmic voice. I would recommend going back to the *Power Windows* album and checking out "The Big Money," "Territories," and especially "Mystic Rhythms" to appreciate the complexity of what Neil was doing at this time.

"Marathon" doesn't really contain a lot in the way of electronic drums or samples, but is a terrific song with a fantastic drum part. Neil juxtaposes a four-on-the-floor bass-drum pattern in the verses with a straight 2-and-4 rock beat in the choruses, and brings a different creative treatment to each verse over the steady bass drum. The guitar solo is in a driving 7, with Neil playing all kinds of different syncopations within the groove.

The last time "Marathon" was performed live was on the *Presto* tour in 1990, and the song was very enthusiastically received when it was brought back for the Time Machine tour. Neil did not change very much in this drum part; the way he performs it now is very close to the way he recorded it. Of course there are slight differences, and as a Rush/Neil fan I always enjoy going back to compare different live versions of the same song, to hear what new ideas (even small ones) Neil may have incorporated.

ANALYSIS:

During the introduction of the song, Neil uses his largest toms, and also incorporates effected samples of his old Tama gong bass drum, which he triggers from the pads above his floor toms on the right. A four-on-the-floor bass drum drives the verse, but what is interesting here is the placement of the snare drum on beat 1, which adds an intensity and drive to this section. The lyrics use running a marathon as a metaphor, and the way the verses are constructed makes them sound like they could be the soundtrack for someone running.

Check out the way Neil incorporates two hands on the hi-hat at the end of the phrases (measure 20). Moving to the second half of the verse, both hands stay on the hi-hat. On the original recording of the song, this pattern was played with the hi-hat more tightly closed, so that the openings were more clearly pronounced, but here I have transcribed this section as it is currently played.

The pre-chorus (bars 40-49) slows the momentum with a half-time feel, then the chorus resolves into "normal" 2-and-4 time, which matches the broad feeling of the melody and lyrics in the chorus. An interesting hi-hat pattern featuring left-hand upbeats is played in the second verse, then the second pre-chorus and chorus maintain the feel and approach established earlier in the song. The fun really begins at measure 103, when the band launches into 7/8 to set up the guitar solo. Geddy lays down some of his trademark funky/fusiony bass playing in this section, and Neil plays off of it with various syncopations between the snare drum and hi-hat. An interesting snare fill at measure 133 leads into the guitar solo section, and Neil begins to get busier with different types of syncopations. He builds the intensity, incorporating busy fills at measures 145, 147-149, and 153.

The dynamic really drops for a quiet interlude starting at measure 158, and then begins to build back up until a peak is reached at measure 166, where Neil is wailing full force on the China cymbal. The transitional fill out of this section (measure 173) works well; it is energetic without being overly complex. This leads to the long out-chorus of the song, in which Neil adds several different types of fills, incorporating snare syncopation against the time (measure 189), triplets introduced into straight time (measure 197), and a two-bar soloistic break (measures 204-205).

MARATHON

MARATHON

MARATHON

MARATHON

MARATHON

CHAPTER 8

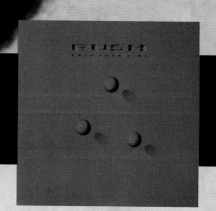

a show of hands

As Neil mentions in the tour book, 1987 was a big year indeed for those interested in his equipment preferences. The candy apple red Tama set had endured three albums and long tours, and was feeling a little road-weary, so Neil set about looking for a new kit. His side-by-side "taste test" of different brands of drums was conducted at The Percussion Center in Fort Wayne, Indiana, and included the following makes: Tama, Yamaha, Ludwig, Sonor, Premier, and Tempus (a Canadian company that makes fiberglass drums). After careful tuning, playing, and comparison, it came down to a neck-and-neck finish between Tama and Ludwig, and in the end Neil felt that the Ludwig drums were just a tad more exciting. The new kit, diagrammed here, was a 1987 Ludwig Super Classic with four-ply maple/poplar shells. Once again it was completely customized by Neal Graham, including the white opalescent finish.

The electronic setup for this tour was much expanded. In a 1987 *Modern Drummer* interview, Neil says: "We were to start working on new material in the fall, and I really wanted to update my electronic outfit as well. I had been watching the progress of digital sampling units for a couple of years, and felt that the time was right to explore that. I spoke with the band's 'technological mentor,' Jim Burgess, told him what I was after, and he recommended the Akai unit, with a Yamaha MIDI controller. I decided to stay with the latest Simmons pads, as I like the feel of them. The sounds are digitally stored on those little 3-1/2" computer disks, and once you put them into the Akai's RAM memory, you can edit and change them at will without affecting the original sample. Assigning them to different pads is a simple affair, and you can copy from the RAM to a new disk to create new setups and safety copies. With the Yamaha MIDI controller, you can create 'chains,' which allow you to change programs with the flick of a footswitch. For example, in one of the new songs on which we're working as I write, I play an African drum setup for the verses, and then click to a setup of my acoustic Tama drums, sampled from 'Grand Designs,' for the choruses." It was clear that Neil was sold on the benefits of electronic drums and MIDI technology.

The number of Simmons pads on this setup expanded to six, and with the continued advancement of technology, the orchestra bells (aka glockenspiel) and temple blocks were retired. However, between all of the Simmons pads and the addition of a MalletKAT MIDI controller, Neil had exact samples of all of these retired percussion instruments to choose from. Other interesting changes at this time included a switch from concert toms in the higher register to all closed toms (which gave Neil a more uniform sound), and a temporary reduction in the number of China cymbals on the kit to two.

From the Hold Your Fire tour book, Neil writes:

Well, lots of Big News in the equipment department this year, for those of you who are interested in such things. When I decided last year that I wanted to get a new set of drums, I went about it in a very methodical way. This time I wanted to be absolutely sure that I was using the best-sounding drums there were. So I went down to The Percussion Center in Fort Wayne, and we tried out six different makes of drums, side by side and with the same heads and tuning. The result was a new set of Ludwig drums—the ones which sounded the most lively and exciting. A similar "A-B" comparison confirmed the effectiveness of the vibra-fibing treatment, and that process of a thin layer of fiberglass has been applied to the inside of the shells.

When Geddy saw the color I had chosen for them, he asked: "What ever possessed you?" Well, I'm not sure about that, but it's another "hot rod" finish like the red ones, this time a combination of white opalescent, with a few "flip-flop" sparkles, and a little hint of pink.

Just different, that's all.

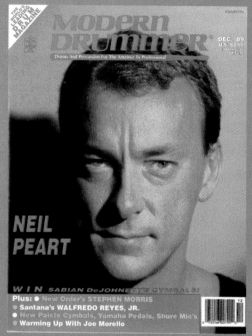

The hardware, which has been brass-plated, is a combination of Premier, Tama, and Pearl fittings, while the cymbals are by Avedis Zildjian, with the exception of the Chinese ones which come from Wuhan province in China. The venerable Slingerland "Artist" snare drums remain, as do the Pro-Mark 747 drumsticks.

Big News in the electronics department as well—the Simmons pads now trigger an Akai digital sampler through a Yamaha MIDI controller. This has expanded my range of available percussion sounds enormously, allowing me to have absolutely any sound available at the flick of a stick or the kick of a switch. Nice. I've also added a KAT keyboard percussion unit, which again gives me all of the keyboard percussion sounds in a neat little package.

In the "traditional" percussion domain, there are temple blocks, timbale, crotales, a Tama gong bass drum, cowbells, and wind chimes.

What else was I going to say?
I forget.
Oh well.

Author's note: As the photos and diagram demonstrate, although Neil mentions using temple blocks, crotales, and chimes, ultimately he did not take these instruments on the tour, and used electronic samples of their sounds instead.

DRUM SETUP

Drums:

Ludwig Super Classic in custom white-with-pink-sparkle finish, with the inside of shells vibra-fibed

1. 14x24 bass drum
2. 5.5x14 "Old Faithful" Slingerland Artist snare drum
3. 5.5x6 concert tom
4. 9x6 tom
5. 9x8 tom
6. 9x10 tom
7. 8x12 tom
8. 9x13 tom
9. 12x15 tom
10. 16x18 floor tom
11. 14x22 Tama gong bass drum
12. 5x14 Slingerland Artist snare drum
13. 6.5x13 Tama brass timbale
14. 14x18 bass drum

Cymbals:

Zildjian (except Wuhan)

A. 13" New Beat Hi-Hats
B. 20" Medium Thin Crash
C. 16" Medium Thin Crash
D. 10" Splash
E. 16" Medium Thin Crash
F. 8" Splash
G. 22" Ping Ride
H. 18" Medium Thin Crash
I. 18" Wuhan Chinese
J. 18" Pang
K. 18" Medium Thin Crash
L. 13" New Beat Hi-Hats
M. 22" Ping Ride
N. 16" Medium Thin Crash
O. 20" Wuhan Chinese

Percussion & Electronics:

aa. MalletKAT electronic percussion controller
bb. Simmons SDS-5 tom module
cc. Simmons SDS-5 snare module
dd. cowbells

Additional Electronics:
Yamaha KX-76 MIDI controller
Akai 900 samplers
Shark pedals
(trigger for electronics)

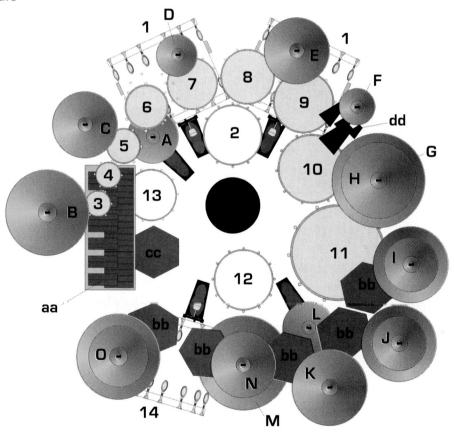

Time Stand Still

Taken from the *Hold Your Fire* album (1987), "Time Stand Still" is a detailed drum part that perfectly displays the high level of Neil's arrangement and orchestration skills. Each groove and fill is carefully thought out and fits so well with the song that it becomes an integral part of the composition.

In the 1980s keyboards and synthesizers became a prinicipal element of the band's sound. The albums *Signals* (1982), *Grace Under Pressure* (1984), *Power Windows* (1985), *Hold Your Fire* (1987), and (to a lesser degree) *Presto* (1989) all feature synthesized sounds in a central role. In order to perform this material, all three members of the band began triggering different samples to reproduce the parts live. Since that time, Rush has always been known as a band on the forefront of music technology.

The use of new musical technology meant one major thing to Neil: electronic drums! Starting with the *Grace Under Pressure* tour in 1984, and on every tour since, Neil has used an electronic drumset facing the opposite direction from his main kit, installed on a rotating riser so that he always faces the audience. While the rotating riser and second kit add a very cool visual element to the show, the reason for their introduction was so that Neil could reproduce the electronic sounds on the albums. His electronic setup has evolved from early Simmons drums in the '80s to state-of-the-art Roland V-Drums today, with enough pads reachable on his main drumset that he only used the rear kit for his drum solo on the Time Machine tour.

In live performance, although Rush uses time-sensitive samples, they are all triggered in real time, and the band does not play to a click. This presents one of the biggest challenges for Neil in live performance (which was discussed on the DVD): maintaining the correct tempo so that when these samples enter, the band does not have to speed up or slow down to accommodate the tempo of the sample. This requires strict attention to and control of the tempo.

In "Time Stand Still," Neil plays a creative groove during the chorus where he uses two "clock tick" sounds that match the lyrical theme. One of these sounds is on a pad reachable by his left hand, while the other is played by his left foot on the electronic pedal to the left of his hi-hat pedal. Other sounds that Neil triggers in this song include a gated reverb effect on the snare drum, castanets, and sound effects.

ANALYSIS:

The introductory guitar theme of the song has seven beats, written out here as a bar of 4/4 and a bar of 3/4. There are some interesting fills in bars 3-6 which were played on timbales on the album, but which Neil has transposed to his highest toms. The second of these fills was inspired by Phil Collins. Interestingly, Neil tells the story that he spent hours trying to learn this particular lick up to tempo, finally mastering it with much admiration of Collins' chops, only to discover years later that Phil had recorded this rhythm with the tape slowed down!

Measures 9-24 are the first verse, and the groove is a straight rock beat, but with carefully placed hi-hat openings and slight snare fills (often with flams) that punctuate the lyrics. Neil also utilizes his signature ride pattern to generate lift going into the choruses (see, for instance, bars 25-26).

The chorus groove is a real point of drumming interest in this song. Here's how it breaks down: The beat is a two-bar phrase in which Neil's right hand plays upbeats on the ride cymbal, while his feet play the downbeats (1, 2, 3, 4) on bass drum and foot hi-hat. However, on beat 3 of the first bar of every two, his left foot moves from the hi-hat to the electronic pedal on the left to trigger one of the "clock tick" sounds, and then moves right back. This can take awhile to master. The left hand then moves around the kit, playing the rest of the accents, as well as the second "clock tick." The only time the right hand leaves the ride cymbal is to play a pad to trigger the reverb sound on beat 4 of every second bar. A truly masterful and creative groove! (Note: It is possible to play this groove without electronics by setting up two wood blocks or LP Jam Blocks to your left, and playing the note Neil plays with his left foot as a left-hand accent.)

Other points of interest include the flowing two-hand 16th-note groove Neil plays in the post-chorus (measures 43-50). During this groove, his left hand moves from the hi-hat to the MalletKAT to trigger the castanet sound. There are also two bridge-type sections in 7/4 (starting at bars 115 and 136, respectively) which can be tricky to understand unless you count through them the first few times. Finally, check out the wonderfully phrased, melodic tom fills in measures 104, 147, 155 and 163.

TIME STAND STILL

Block Sample

Block Sample

Reverb Snare Sample

TIME STAND STILL

TIME STAND STILL

Electronic Drum Sample

TIME STAND STILL

TIME STAND STILL

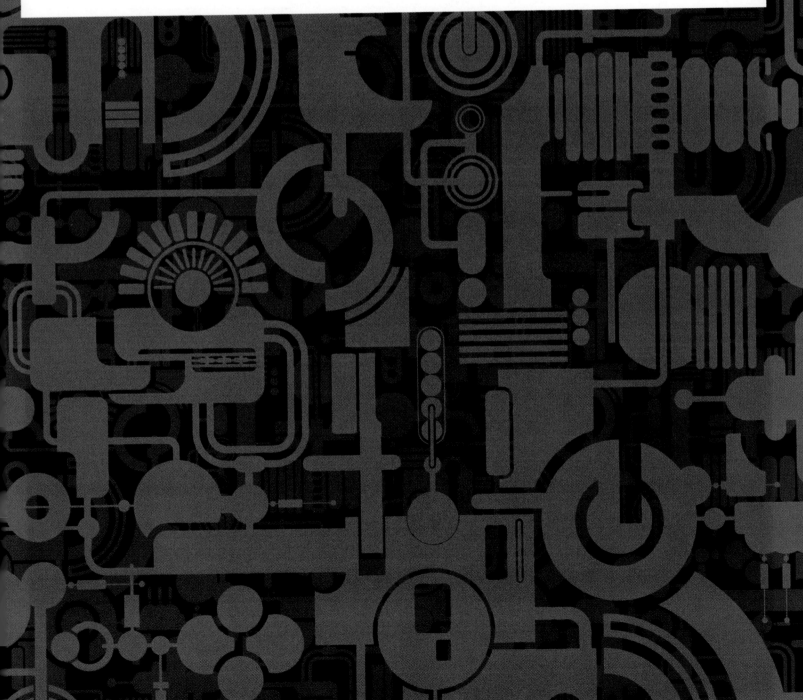

slight rit. - - - - - - - -

CHAPTER 9

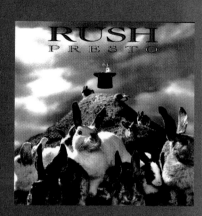

The drumset used for the *Presto* album and tour was the same Ludwig kit as the *Hold Your Fire* album and tour, just refinished in a shade of purple. Neil added two concert toms (5.5"x6" and 5.5"x8"), which were placed over the MalletKAT, to the left of his highest closed toms, but set lower, so they could be reached from the rear kit. The snare drum on the rear kit became a 13" Ludwig piccolo, and the Simmons pads were replaced by ddrum ones.

Many of the percussion instruments formerly in Neil's setup (and sometimes newer samples of them) could be heard on the *Presto* tour in songs like "Xanadu" and "Closer to the Heart." The song "Scars" (from *Presto*) was also played, and required extensive use of sampling, including Neil triggering the snare drum backbeat with his left foot. "Mission," from *Hold Your Fire*, used a mixed marimba/snare drum sound triggered on the MalletKAT, and "Time Stand Still" contained a fair amount of triggering as well.

From the Presto tour book, Neil writes:

Don't be fooled, these are *not* new drums. Nope, they're the same Ludwigs as last time, the ones that used to be pinkish, only now they're a dark, plummy, sort of purplish color (beautifully finished by Paintworks).

Cymbals are all by Avedis Zildjian, except for the Chinese Wuhans, and the brass-plated hardware is a hybrid of what-have-you: Ludwig, Tama, Pearl, Premier, and some custom-made bits from The Percussion Center in Fort Wayne. The gong bass drum comes from Tama, and the cowbells come from Guernsey & Holstein. Sticks are Pro-Mark 747, and heads—always subject to change, just like human ones—are some combination or other of Remo and Evans. I just keep changing my mind—and my heads.

Same with snare drums. That remains an open question, but I'm sure to be using some combination of my old reliable Slingerland, a Solid Percussion piccolo, an old Camco, and/or a Ludwig 13" piccolo (cute little thing).

The electronics are triggered by ddrum pads and Shark foot pedals, driving a Yamaha MIDI controller and an Akai S900 sampler. A KAT MIDI-marimba drives another Akai for all the keyboard percussion parts and various effects.

You know, I was thinking about what my drum kit would look like if I had all the real instruments up there, rather than a box full of floppy disks and a couple of samplers. Picture a stage which contained (in addition to that little ol' drumset): temple blocks, orchestra bells, bell tree, glockenspiel, marimba, various African drums (including ones like "djembe" that I don't even know what it looks like), three tympani, a full symphony orchestra, a "beeper," a big gong, harp, synthesizer, congas, bongos, another timbale, castanets, voice-drums (recorded drum sounds vocalized by *moi*), a big huge sheet of metal, jackhammer, wood block, claves, jingled coins, my old red Tama drum kit, and Count Basie and his band.

Oh sure, it would look great all right, but honestly—where would I put all that stuff? And where would the other two guys stand?

Yeah, you're right; I don't need those guys anyway.

DRUM SETUP

Drums:

Ludwig Super Classic in custom plum finish, with the inside of shells vibra-fibed

1. 14x24 bass drum
2. 5.5x14 "Old Faithful" Slingerland Artist snare drum
3. 5.5x6 concert tom
4. 5.5x8 concert tom
5. 9x6 tom
6. 9x8 tom
7. 9x10 tom
8. 8x12 tom
9. 9x13 tom
10. 12x15 tom
11. 16x18 floor tom
12. 14x22 Tama gong bass drum
13. 5x13 Ludwig piccolo snare drum
14. 6.5x13 Tama brass timbale
15. 14x18 bass drum

Cymbals:

Zildjian (except Wuhan)

A. 13" New Beat Hi-Hats
B. 20" Medium Thin Crash
C. 16" Medium Thin Crash
D. 10" Splash
E. 16" Medium Thin Crash
F. 8" Splash
G. 22" Ping Ride
H. 18" Medium Thin Crash
I. 18" Wuhan Chinese
J. 18" Pang
K. 18" Medium Thin Crash
L. 13" New Beat Hi-Hats
M. 22" Ping Ride
N. 16" Medium Thin Crash
O. 20" Wuhan Chinese

Percussion & Electronics:

aa. MalletKAT electronic percussion controller
bb. ddrum pad
cc. cowbells
dd. wind chimes/bar chimes
ee. Shark pedals (trigger for electronics)

Additional Electronics:
Yamaha KX-76 MIDI controller
Akai 900 samplers

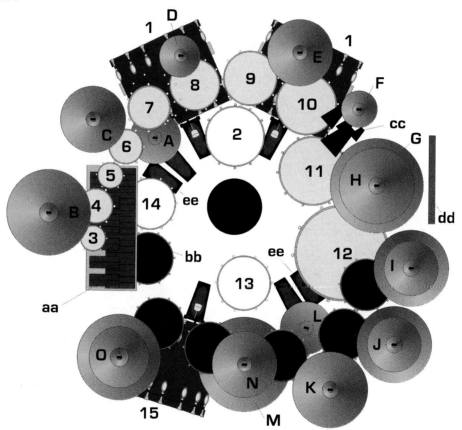

PRESTO

The *Presto* album (1989) came at an interesting juncture for Rush. The band had left Polygram records and signed with Atlantic, and had just released the live album *A Show of Hands*, which allowed the band a bit of time off. According to Neil, the band returned to work fresh and enthused, and this album was not stressful to make. With a new producer and engineer in the fold—Rupert Hine and Stephen Tayler—the sound of the record (in terms of the mix and the sound of the instruments, especially the drums) was quite different, and the musical approach had developed to a point where the synthesizers, sampling, and keyboards were less of a focal point than on the previous three albums.

Presto has some very interesting and challenging drum parts, notably those in "Show Don't Tell" (the best-known song from the album, and the one that has been performed live most frequently), and "Scars," which has a groove based on an African rhythm with a paradiddle sticking. In order to execute the African rhythm properly, Neil triggered the snare backbeat on 2 and 4 with his left foot. This drum groove was memorable and catchy enough that it survived as part of Neil's drum solos for a couple of tours. *Presto* has not been ignored on recent tours; on the *Vapor Trails* tour (2002), the band brought back "The Pass," and for the Time Machine tour, one of the surprises in the setlist was the title track, "Presto."

"Presto" is more sparse than many other Rush drum parts, but contains some great-sounding and creative ideas to match the somewhat mellow mood of the song. Neil mentions that sometimes when he listens back to older albums, he can remember what he was listening to at that time, and around 1989 he was listening to a lot of Manu Katché. Manu's influence can be heard in some of the two-handed accented hi-hat parts, and in the placement of some of the syncopated snare-drum accents.

ANALYSIS:

This song truly reflects Neil's style: He matches each part of the song with a different approach to the timekeeping. After the opening ensemble figures, the drums lay out (just keeping minimal time on the hi-hat) until measure 20, at which point a groove is introduced that contains sixteenth-note hi-hat with accents on 2 and 4 over a bass-drum part that moves in unison with the bass guitar. The snare drum is omitted.

The section at measure 29 is essentially the chorus of the song, and this section reflects the Manu Katché influence the most. Straight bass drum and hi-hat are punctuated with different accents and syncopations on the snare drum and large toms. The bass-drum pattern adds forward motion, but the lack of a backbeat keeps the energy in check, saving something for later in the song. At measure 47, the second verse builds on the groove presented in the first, but adds more accents on the hi-hat, and incorporates the satellite snare drum on the left side.

After some ensemble figures in measures 55-56, a snare-drum backbeat is finally introduced (this section is still a verse), over a straight-up rock groove that has quite a busy bass drum part. Due to the great camera work on the *Taking Center Stage* DVD, it is easy to see how active Neil's right foot actually is. For many of the transcriptions in this book, we have included bass-drum notes in parentheses (for instance, in measures 60-61), to indicate that a very soft, incidental note is played. If these notes were played loudly, they would probably make the groove sound too busy. Neil uses a traditional bass-drum tuning, with a full head on the front of the drum. Although he gets a huge sound, it is still a traditional sound—there isn't a massive amount of beater click/attack—and this allows Neil to play more notes, in the tradition of many of his early influences such as Keith Moon, without overpowering the groove. As you watch the DVD and study these transcriptions, note the dynamics that occur on Neil's bass drum.

The guitar solo section starting at measure 105 has Neil moving to the ride cymbal, and incorporating his left foot into the groove. This is another interesting aspect of his playing in recent years. Depending on the song and the groove, Neil does different things with his left foot. On some songs (the intro of "Free Will," for instance), his left foot will play only the snare backbeats. On others, he will play straight quarter notes, and on still others, the left foot will play a basic quarter-note feel but will vary and change, adding or subtracting notes, depending on what the other limbs are doing. This is the case in "Presto." It seems obvious that Neil did not specifically design these left-foot parts to play on certain beats, but just relaxes into the groove and allows his left foot to do what is comfortable, and this creates some of these complex rhythms. Keep this in mind when trying some of Neil's grooves. In your personal playing, a different left-foot part might feel more comfortable.

PRESTO

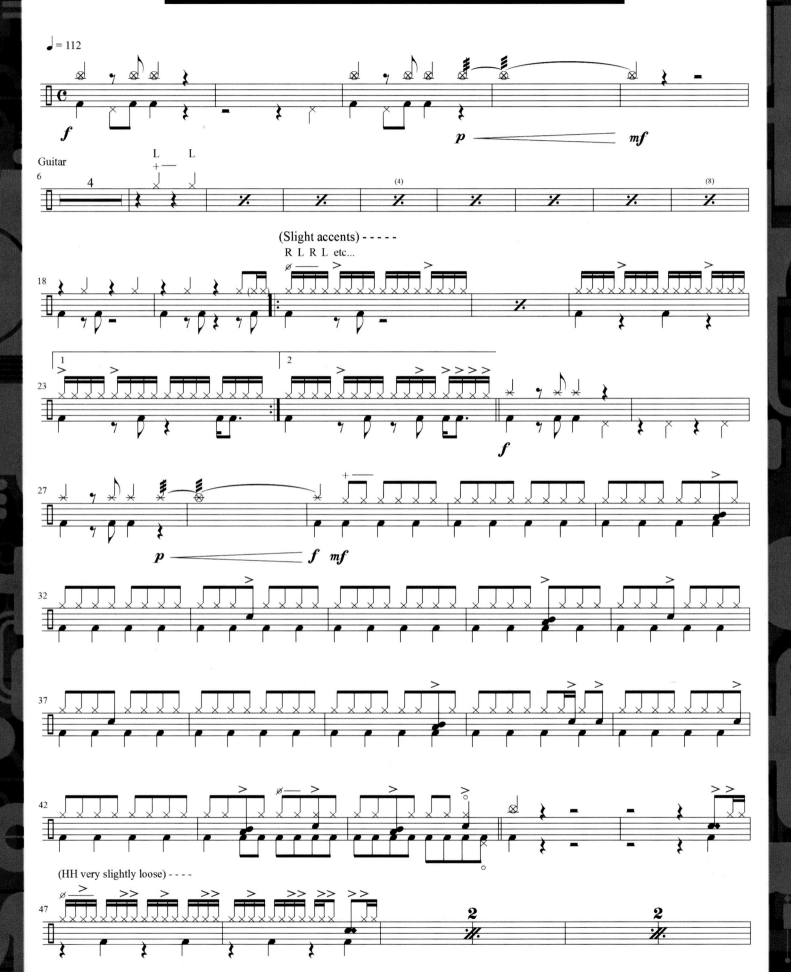

PRESTO

PRESTO

PRESTO

CHAPTER 10

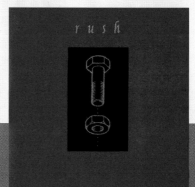

Roll the Bones and Counterparts Tours

(1991-92, 1994)

For *Roll the Bones*, Neil rethought his drum setup for the first time since he had joined Rush. He had always made changes to his setup, but this never involved the arrangement of the basic pieces of his set; in the past it had usually involved adding new pieces, or swapping out various percussion instruments and accessories. This time, major changes were made. First, Neil decided to go from using two bass drums to a single bass drum with a double pedal. Second, he put a floor tom on the left. Finally, he switched to smaller tom-tom sizes. This made for a much more compact basic drumset (although as you can see from the diagram, it was still a pretty huge kit).

Neil used the same setup for both the *Roll the Bones* and *Counterparts* tours; the only real change was having the drums refinished from "Blue Shadow" to "Dark Cherry." Otherwise, all the drums, cymbals, and electronics stayed the same, the only exceptions being the addition of a Dauz pad—placed at the rear, under the wind chimes—and a tambourine for the *Counterparts* tour. The diagram shows the *Roll the Bones* tour kit.

Through all the various equipment changes of the previous eighteen years, Neil's cymbal setup had changed very little. He kept the same 22-inch Ping Ride until he left Zildjian. The other sizes and models also stayed remarkably consistent. It is interesting to note that Zildjian catalogs of the time listed all of Neil's crashes as "Medium Thin," however his current Sabian Paragon line is more of a "Medium" weight.

NEIL PEART

Ludwig Super Classic Series

For a Neil Peart Poster, send $3 to Ludwig Industries, Neil Peart Poster, P.O. Box 310, Elkhart, IN 46515

Ludwig

From the Roll the Bones tour book, Neil writes:

On the day we began setting up for the writing stage of *Roll the Bones*, I stood in the little studio and watched Larry putting my drums together. It occurred to me that I'd been using the same basic setup for years now, and maybe it was time for a rethink—time to make some changes, take some chances. Just putting the drums in different places might alter my approach to them, push me in some new directions.

So we started moving the toms around, putting the floor tom under my left hand, and shifting the others down one position, placing the 15" where the floor tom used to be, the 13" where the 15" used to be, and like that. This gave me some new rhythmic possibilities, new ways to construct fills, and even familiar patterns would sound different.

Also, I wanted to try using a single bass drum, with two pedals—to eliminate a big resonating chamber (the other bass drum) which I hardly ever used. I also decided to try a different size: 22" rather than 24".

So we did all that, and it was good...

My first set of Ludwigs had survived five years of hard labor: recording *Hold Your Fire*, *Presto*, and *Roll the Bones*, as well as two long tours which included the recording of *A Show of Hands*. They'd gone from pretty-in-pink to plum-crazy, and still sounded good, but maybe it was time to give them a rest. Time for a new kit.

And here it is: Ludwigs once again, in their "Blue Shadow" finish, with the brass-plating and "vibra-fibing" coordinated by The Percussion Center in Fort Wayne. Other than the above-named changes, the setup remains the same; Zildjian cymbals (but for the two Chinese Wuhans), Slingerland snare, assorted cowbells, and Tama gong bass drum. In the "back forty," we find the Ludwig 13" piccolo snare, 18" bass drum, plus ddrum pads, Shark pedals, and KAT MIDI-marimba triggering Akai samplers. Remo heads are punished by Pro-Mark "Signature" sticks. And that's what's new in the toy box—I mean *tool* box!

DRUM SETUP

Drums:

Ludwig Super Classic in Blue Shadow finish, with the inside of shells vibra-fibed; brass-plated hardware

1. 16x22 bass drum
2. 5.5x14 "Old Faithful" Slingerland Artist snare drum
3. 5.5x6 tom
4. 5.5x8 tom
5. 8x10 tom
6. 8x12 tom
7. 9x13 tom
8. 16x16 floor tom
9. 14x22 Tama gong bass drum
10. 5x13 Ludwig piccolo snare drum
11. 14x18 bass drum
12. 12x15 floor tom
13. 3x14 Remo Legato piccolo snare

Cymbals:

Zildjian (except Wuhan)

A. 13" New Beat Hi-Hats
B. 20" Medium Thin Crash
C. 16" Medium Thin Crash
D. 10" Splash
E. 16" Medium Thin Crash
F. 8" Splash
G. 22" Ping Ride
H. 18" Medium Thin Crash
I. 18" Wuhan Chinese
J. 18" Pang
K. 18" Medium Thin Crash
L. 13" New Beat Hi-Hats
M. 22" Ping Ride
N. 16" Medium Thin Crash
O. 20" Wuhan Chinese

Percussion & Electronics:

aa. MalletKAT electronic percussion controller
bb. ddrum pad
cc. cowbells
dd. wind chimes/bar chimes
ee. Shark pedals (trigger for electronics)

Additional Electronics:
Yamaha KX-76 MIDI controller
Akai 900 samplers

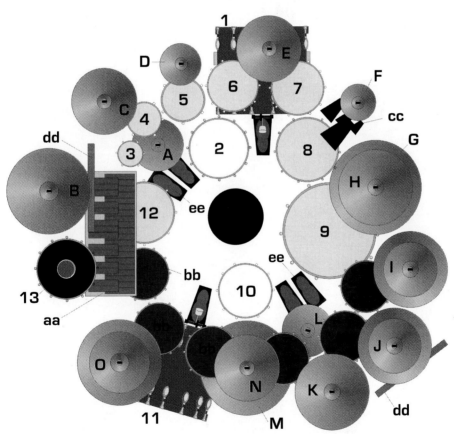

Bravado

In terms of Rush's sound, *Roll the Bones*, released in 1992, picked up where *Presto* (1989) left off. On this record Neil's parts seemed to be chosen above all to fit the songs, and without much regard for flash, although there are some challenging parts on the album. The instrumental "Where's My Thing?" employed bombastic fills yet hinted at Neil's future fascination with jazz, and "Heresy" took rhythms Neil heard in West Africa and crafted them into an amazingly creative, musical, and fun drum part (one of my favorites, actually). *Roll the Bones* also contained three songs that would become staples of Rush's concert performances in the coming years: "Dreamline," "Roll the Bones," and "Bravado." In addition, "Ghost of a Chance" was a deep cut that was brought back for the second half of the *Snakes & Arrows* tour in 2008.

Although "Bravado" was ultimately struck from the setlist of the Time Machine tour, we had filmed a wonderful take of Neil rehearsing the song during our first shoot for *Taking Center Stage*, and felt that it should be included on the DVD, both because it is a favorite song of Neil's and because it has such an interesting drum part. It is included in the book for the same reasons, and because *Roll the Bones* is an important album that shouldn't be overlooked in any review of Rush and Neil's history.

"Bravado" builds dynamically from a simple and bare hi-hat groove to one of Neil's most complex multi-surface beats, using voices covering the entire lateral spread of the kit. This drum part is a wonderful example of how creative and active drumming can lift a song in an effective and musically appropriate way. One of the best things that can be said about Neil Peart's drumming is that his parts are inseparable from the songs they were written for. This is a high musical compliment.

ANALYSIS:

"Bravado" starts out innocently enough, using a straightforward two-hands-on-the-hi-hat rock groove, which breaks down into just hi-hat and bass drum at bar 17. Pay close attention to the dynamic shifts in this song; they are essential to getting the drum part to feel right and fit with the tune. At bar 19, Neil uses hi-hat accents and splash cymbal in a characteristically appropriate way to accent a vocal phrase.

The groove at measure 37 is not terribly difficult to play, but is terrifically creative in its composition (try to think of another song that uses this beat!). This groove not only works perfectly for this section, but also sets up the introduction of the double floor toms at bar 45. In this groove, Neil's left hand plays the left floor tom and his right hand plays the right floor tom. This "bilateral tom" theme becomes a major feature of the drum part in this song, and is maintained even when Neil begins to introduce other voices and accents into the groove. Next, during the guitar solo (starting at bar 57), Neil places a simple yet memorable fill at the end of every two bars.

The climax of the drumming in "Bravado" occurs at measure 93, where Neil keeps the double floor tom theme going as his right hand moves to the ride-cymbal bell. The left hand continues to play the offbeats on the hi-hat, as well as the syncopated snare drum accents that occur in measures 95, 97, 102, and 104. The right hand plays between the ride bell and the snare drum (for the main backbeats), and this is all executed over a bass-drum pattern that essentially keeps the same figure from the previous section. The groove itself is very challenging, and the ability to be able to insert the fills and crash cymbal accents that occur throughout the part are even more difficult. When learning this groove, work it up to tempo and get comfortable with it before trying to add the fills and other details.

BRAVADO

BRAVADO

BRAVADO

LEAVE THAT THING ALONE!

This song, from *Counterparts* (1993), is one of a long line of fantastic Rush instrumentals, and one that the band clearly enjoys playing. (It was performed on the tours for *Counterparts*, *Test for Echo*, and *Vapor Trails*, and then brought back again for the Time Machine tour.) It was nominated for a Grammy in 1994 for Best Rock Instrumental Performance (losing to Pink Floyd's "Marooned"). *Counterparts* is an excellent and diverse album, containing a number of memorable tracks. "Nobody's Hero" is essentially a ballad, but with an involved and highly developed drum part, and "Double Agent" is quite complex both in the chops required to play the part, and in its timing and arrangement.

There is an interesting sequenced "loop" of a synthesized bass sound underneath the introduction of "Leave That Thing Alone!", and when Rush plays this tune live, this sequence is triggered first, before the band enters. This gives Neil a chance to lock down the tempo, because Rush never employs a click live (so Neil must play in time with certain triggered sequences based on only hearing the actual sequence, and relying on his own internal time.) The drum groove and sequenced synth part form the bottom, and Geddy actually plays the melody of the introduction on the bass.

During the second verse of the song, there is a unique drum groove utilizing the toms that is based on a rhythm Neil heard in Nigeria. This groove is very difficult to play without Neil's specific setup, because the first two notes played on the left floor tom lead immediately up to notes on the highest toms. If you have a conventional kit with only one floor tom on the right, the distance across the kit is quite far to cover. In addition, Neil plays a tambourine sound with his left foot on a trigger pedal. The tambourine sound actually has a strong presence on *Counterparts*. It is played using a foot trigger on this song, "Animate," and "Nobody's Hero," and an actual mounted tambourine is played with the right hand on "Cold Fire." Interestingly, after this album, Neil didn't use the tambourine sound again on any songs, but did incorporate it as the left-foot sound in his drum solo while playing the Max Roach motif "The Drum Also Waltzes," and has continued to use it in that application.

ANALYSIS:

The opening groove of "Leave That Thing Alone!" is a straight, driving rock groove with some syncopated bass-drum figures. When watching the *Taking Center Stage* DVD, you will notice how hard Neil hits the snare drum. There is a certain definition that comes from this style of playing; it allows Neil to play busy parts that still come across in larger arenas (where busy drum patterns can easily sound muddy). Neil does admit that he hits "as hard as he can" but he doesn't sacrifice relaxation to do this, which is evidenced by the fact that even after years of touring, he does not have any drumming-related injuries.

The Nigerian-inspired groove comes in at measure 26. Notice the interesting orchestration (discussed above) and the melodic quality of the pattern. This is one of many interesting "African"-sounding grooves that Neil has recorded. Some of them, like this one, came from actual African rhythms ("Heresy," from *Roll the Bones*, has a groove that was inspired by a rhythm Neil heard in Togo), while others, like "High Water" from *Hold Your Fire* or "Territories" from *Power Windows*, sound tribal but without a specific indigenous African reference. Either way, these are some memorable, exciting, and fun grooves.

A bridge section/interlude with a softer dynamic begins at measure 39, with a shift into 3/4 time and Neil playing a ride/hi-hat figure that sounds like a straightened-out jazz beat. An alternating bass-drum/hi-hat foot pattern then enters, while Neil pays various syncopations over it with his ride cymbal and snare drum. This section builds into measure 67, which features a straight-up groove (although in 6/4) with the bass drum playing driving eighth notes.

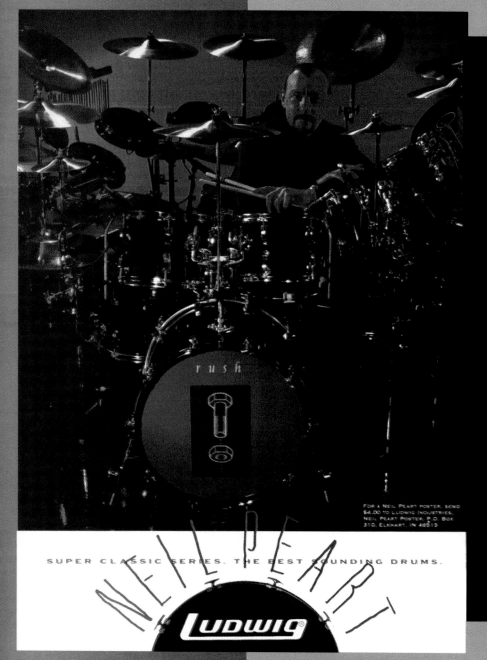

One of Neil's most interesting and rhythmically bizarre drum breaks is played in measures 102-103. The function of this break is to create a transition between the preceding heavy/distorted guitar groove and the return to the reprise of the smoother opening section. Neil achieves this by using all of the same voices from the Nigerian beat, but in an entirely different rhythmic construction. Again, this fill is customized to Neil's kit, with the bass-drum triplet leading to a flam on the left floor tom, and then jumping up quickly to the highest tom. The 32nd-note figure in the second measure of the fill is similar to the rhythm in the first drum break in "YYZ," but here, the way Neil moves his left hand up to the 13" tom "disguises" the figure somewhat, making it very difficult to figure out and phrase correctly. Also notice the incorporation of the two electronic sampled sounds into this break. These "industrial"-sounding samples also occur in the Nigerian groove and in a few other places in the song.

LEAVE THAT THING ALONE!

LEAVE THAT THING ALONE!

LEAVE THAT THING ALONE!

LEAVE THAT THING ALONE!

CHAPTER 11

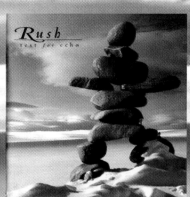

TEST FOR ECHO TOUR
(1996-97)

After seeing the incredible results for drummer colleagues such as Dave Weckl and Steve Smith, Neil took a sabbatical from Rush in 1995 to study with drum teaching legend Freddie Gruber. During this time, Neil reevaluated and reinvented many of the aspects of his playing style (documenting much of what he learned on the *Neil Peart: A Work in Progress* instructional video package). He moved himself a little further back from the drums, relaxed his stroke, switched to traditional grip (a change that would prove temporary), and reconfigured his drumset to accommodate a more relaxed approach (a change that would prove permanent). He also switched drum brands again, to Drum Workshop (DW), which was fast becoming one of the world's leading drum manufacturers in the late 1990s.

Most of the changes to Neil's setup revolved around the major change of moving the ride cymbal into a more comfortable position (partially over the bass drum, where most jazz drummers have it), thereby changing his core setup to the basic four-piece configuration used by Buddy Rich, Gene Krupa, John Bonham, Max Roach, Charlie Watts, and countless others. The mounted toms were then shifted up one position, and since the splash cymbal/cowbell stand had formerly been in the space that the ride now occupied, it was moved far out of the way to the left, above the MalletKAT. There was now also additional space over the ride cymbal, so a new voice was added: a closed hi-hat (with splash on top). Neil now used three floor toms on the right, including an aerially mounted 18-inch drum (filling the same musical role as the gong drum). The basic positions of crash, splash, and China cymbals did not really change.

Although Neil continued to use the same type of pads and samplers as on previous tours, the conception of the electronic setup began to evolve, with the incorporation of three additional pads that Neil could reach from the front kit. By using these, and the left-foot trigger pedal, Neil could play the majority of the songs in the setlist (even those requiring electronics) from the front kit. The rear kit contained the same basic setup as on previous tours (still using acoustic snare drum, bass drum, and cymbals) and was used less, but was given a creative touch on the *Test for Echo* tour with double 18-inch bass drums.

Neil also switched at this time to using DW hardware exclusively, including their pedals and hi-hat stands, and thinner Remo drumheads than he had used in the past (coated Ambassadors over the entire kit, to be exact).

From the Test for Echo tour book, Neil writes:

The drums? Well, they're Stewarts, of course, with an 18" Capri bass drum I got in a trade from my friend, and featuring the finest Ajax cymbals from Japan. (As my colleague Lerxst pointed out, those were the days when "Made in Japan" really *meant* something — none of your quality materials and meticulous workmanship then, boy!)

Nowadays, although my drums are red sparkle once again (in the spirit of my "starting over" drumming-wise), there are a few more of them, and they are American-made DWs, right down to the pedals, stands, and even (shock, horror!) the snare drum. "Old Number One," the Slingerland wood-shell snare I've used since forever, has been retired from the field after a glorious career, and a couple of fine DW snares have taken its place.

The toms are 8", 10", 12", 13", 15" (two), 16", and 18", the bass drum is a 22" (with a pair of 18" "cannons" on the back setup), mixed in with two 13" piccolo snares, Akai samplers driven by ddrum pads, KAT MIDI-marimba, and Shark pedals, and the usual selection of cowbells and wind chimes.

The heads are Remo white-coated Ambassadors (just for a change), and the cymbals are by Zildjian, except for one Chinese Wuhan. My sticks are the Pro-Mark 747 "Signature" model, in Japanese white oak.

My teacher for the past couple of years has been Freddie Gruber, and I would like to thank him for leading me down the paths of righteousness.

DRUM SETUP

Drums:

Drum Workshop FinishPly (maple shells, no vibra-fibing) in Blood Red Sparkle finish

1. 16x22 bass drum
2. 6x14 DW Edge snare drum (maple/brass)
3. 7x8 tom
4. 7x10 tom
5. 8x12 tom
6. 9x13 tom
7. 12x15 floor tom
8. 16x16 floor tom
9. 16x18 floor tom
10. 3.5x13 snare drum
11. 16x18 bass drum
12. 13x15 floor tom
13. 3.5x13 snare drum

Cymbals:

Zildjian (except Wuhan)

A. 13" New Beat Hi-Hats
B. 10" Splash
C. 20" Medium Thin Crash
D. 16" Medium Thin Crash
E. 10" Splash
F. 16" Medium Thin Crash
G. 22" Ping Ride
H. 14" New Beat Hi-Hats
I. 8" Splash
J. 18" Medium Thin Crash
K. 20" China Boy Low
L. 18" Wuhan Chinese
M. 13" New Beat Hi-Hats
N. 18" Medium Thin Crash
O. 22" Ping Ride
P. 16" Medium Thin Crash
Q. 20" Wuhan Chinese

Percussion & Electronics:

aa. MalletKAT electronic percussion controller
bb. cowbells
cc. ddrum pad
dd. Shark pedals (trigger for electronics)
ee. Dauz pad
ff. wind chimes/bar chimes

Additional Electronics:
Yamaha KX-76 MIDI controller
Akai 900 samplers

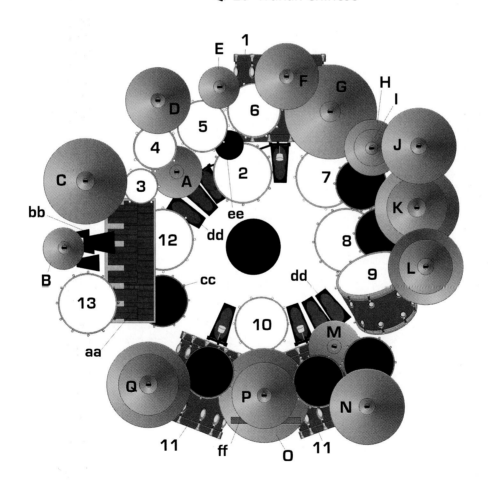

CHAPTER 12

'The Great Paragon Prize'

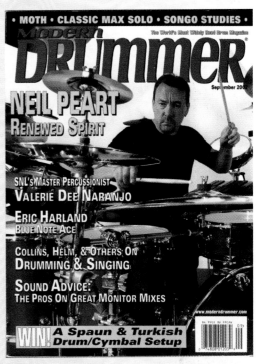

After the long hiatus and return documented in Neil's book *Ghost Rider*, Neil stayed with all of the improvements and changes he had made with Freddie Gruber, but returned to playing matched grip. This was probably for two reasons: First, the matched grip is more efficient and effective for loud rock playing (look at the tape all over Stewart Copeland's hands in an old Police DVD for proof), and second, as Billy Cobham was fond of pointing out, matched grip is much more efficient for getting around the modern large drumset. So, it was back to matched grip, but otherwise the approach and drumset configuration from *Test for Echo* remained the same.

One interesting piece of physical proof showing how much Neil's technique had improved was the fact that, aside from his snare drum, he rarely ever changed his heads on this tour. Because he was using so much more rebound in his stroke, the heads were resonating more freely, not denting or wearing, and not losing their tone. Therefore, Neil and tech Lorne "Gump" Wheaton decided to leave the same heads on.

The only major equipment change for this tour involved switching to Roland V-Drums and their TD-10 brain. V-Drums represented such a major jump in drum technology that they quickly became the professional standard for electronic drums, and Roland also produced the first professionally effective electronic cymbals (V-Cymbals), which Neil now used, thereby converting his rear kit to a completely electronic setup.

In addition to all the benefits these changes brought to Neil, they also brought a major perk to the concert-going fans: Whether Neil was playing his front kit or the rear one, you could now see him much better!

From the Vapor Trails tour book, Neil writes:

The drums are made by DW, with a custom red sparkle finish—same as the last tour. (DW offered to build me a new set, but these ones still sounded great, so I decided to keep them.)

The bass drum is 22", the toms are 8", 10", 12", 13", 15" (two), 16", and 18". The current favorite snare drum is a 5"x14" DW Craviatto, and I'm also using a 13" DW piccolo snare, miscellaneous LP cowbells, and DW pedals and hardware.

Out back, and hidden all around, are Roland V-Drums and trigger pads, accompanying the KAT mallet controller and Shark pedals, all feeding into Roland TD-10 modules with expansion cards, Roland 5080 sampler, line mixer, and MIDI converters.

(I have no idea what any of that means.)

Drumheads are Remo white-coated Ambassadors, and cymbals are Avedis Zildjian: 8" splash, two 10" splashes, 13" hi-hats, 14" X-hats, two 16" crashes, 18" crash, 20" crash, 22" ride, 20" Low China, and an 18" Chinese Wuhan.

(That sort of thing I understand better—you just hit them with sticks. Pro-Mark 747 "Signature" ones, in this case.)

Someone has also written at the end of this list that I have "a really great drum tech." That would be Lorne Wheaton, better known as "Gump." Or is that "Grump"? Time will tell...

DRUM SETUP

Drums:

Drum Workshop FinishPly (maple shells, no vibra-fibing) in Blood Red Sparkle finish

1. 16x22 bass drum
2. 5x14 DW Craviotto snare drum (maple) (or 6.5x14 Edge)
3. 7x8 tom
4. 7x10 tom
5. 8x12 tom
6. 9x13 tom
7. 12x15 floor tom
8. 16x16 floor tom
9. 16x18 floor tom
10. 13x15 floor tom
11. 3.5x13 snare drum

Cymbals:

Zildjian (except Wuhan)

A. 13" New Beat Hi-Hats
B. 10" Splash
C. 20" Medium Thin Crash
D. 16" Medium Thin Crash
E. 10" Splash
F. 16" Medium Thin Crash
G. 22" Ping Ride
H. 14" New Beat Hi-Hats
I. 8" Splash
J. 18" Medium Thin Crash
K. 20" China Boy Low
L. 18" Wuhan Chinese

Percussion & Electronics:

aa. MalletKAT electronic percussion controller
bb. cowbells
cc. Roland V-Drum
dd. Roland V-Cymbal
ee. Roland V-Hi-Hat
ff. Shark pedals (trigger for electronics)
gg. Dauz pad

Additional Electronics:
Roland TD-10 V-Drum brains (2
Roland 5080 sampler
Roland MIDI converter

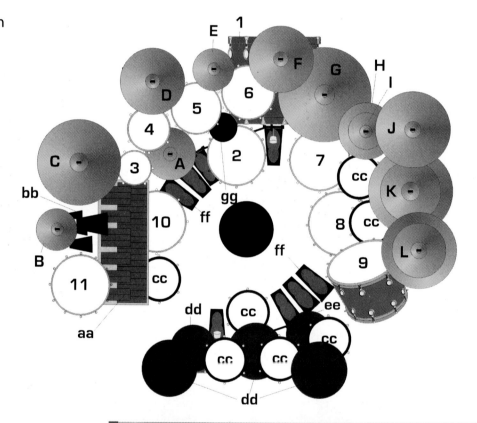

CHAPTER 13

30th Anniversary World Tour

R30 Tour
(2004)

The drum configuration and sizes on the R30 tour (named for Rush's 30th anniversary) did not change from Neil's previous DW setup, but all of the actual instruments were new. By far the biggest (and to some, most surprising) change was that Neil made the switch to Sabian cymbals. He had the occasion to play a stock set of Sabians while preparing for the Canadian Rocks for Toronto benefit concert in 2003, after which he expressed to Sabian his interest in using their products. The result was a high-end line of cymbals designed by Sabian to meet Neil's specifications, which were then marketed to the public as the Paragon line, Neil's signature cymbals. The line is limited in production to the exact models that Neil actually uses (for instance, Neil uses a 22-inch ride, so that is the only ride size offered in the Paragon line). This series has subsequently gone on to become one of Sabian's best sellers.

The new R30 DW drum kit was Neil's most "tricked out" yet, with a custom finish that incorporated logos and symbols from past Rush albums and songs, and (probably the ultimate in drum "bling") 24-karat gold-plated hardware (down to every last tension rod). DW manufactured 30 exact replicas of this drumset, which were sold to the public (with a full set of Paragon cymbals and normal tripods on the cymbal stands, of course).

After the R30 tour was over, Neil's kit was displayed at the Sabian booth at NAMM (the world's largest music trade convention), where it drew big crowds, and was then sent on a North American clinic tour where tech Lorne Wheaton and Sabian cymbal specialist Mark Love (or other personnel) would discuss the setup and explain what went into manufacturing it—marking the first time in history that a drumset (without its illustrious owner) was the star on a national drum clinic tour.

Just about everything in my workshop is new and different this tour—everything but the drummer, really. (And the equally aging, but invaluable, drum tech, Lorne "Gump" Wheaton.) Even the drum riser had to be rebuilt, after it was demolished during load-out after the Rio de Janeiro show

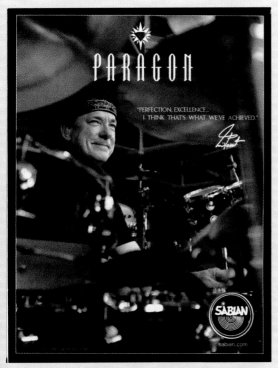

(fortunately the last show of the *Vapor Trails* tour). Upended on a flatbed truck, the riser was being ferried to the semi-trailers outside the stadium, when the driver failed to notice that his load was higher than the exit. Just like in a cartoon, the whole big assembly flew off the back and went "boom."

After that Rio show (I've been dying to tell this story somewhere), we also had to leave behind the carpet that covered the stage (40' by 24', with the *Vapor Trails* logo in the middle). It had absorbed so much rain over those three shows in Brazil, it was too heavy to ship back to Canada. Apparently it finally dried out, decorated a Brazilian home awhile, then appeared on eBay.

But I digress.

The biggest news is the cymbals. In September of 2003, I had the fascinating experience of visiting the Sabian factory in Meductic, New Brunswick, and working with cymbal master Mark Love on the design of my own line of cymbals, called Paragon. The results have been extremely gratifying, first in how well they work for me, and second in how well they've been received by other musicians. I play a 22" ride, 20", 18", and two 16" crashes, 13" hi-hats, 14" "X-hats," 8" and 10" splashes, and 19" and 20" China types.

The drums are also brand, spanking new, a special "30th Anniversary" kit created for me by the good people at DW. As we worked together on the design, we aimed to create the drumset equivalent of the "dream cars" displayed at auto shows, a showpiece that was also the ultimate expression of craftsmanship. John Good carefully selected the woods and laminates, even the grain direction, for maximum tonality, and the shells, as always, were timbre-matched to complement—and compliment—each other musically. Additional thanks to Don and Garrison for their overview and detail work, and the finish was developed with master painter Louie and transfer-designer Javier, partly inspired by Keith Moon's "Pictures of Lily" kit, to represent the "dream drums" of my youth.

The sizes are the same as the old red sparkle kit, 22" bass drum, toms 8", 10", 12", 13", two 15", 16", and 18". I have been favoring either the DW "Edge" model snare drum (indoors) or the DW "Solid Shell" (outdoors). The hardware is plated in 24-karat gold this time, rather than brass, and the heads are DW's own design, which have lovely feel and resonance.

DW also put together custom shells for the Roland V-Drums, to give a nice completion to the electronic side of the shop, which also includes a MalletKAT, KAT trigger pedals, and a Dauz pad, all running through a Roland XV-5080 sampler and Glyph X-Project hard drives.

Bringing it all back to basics, and keeping it real (not to say primitive), I continue to beat on all that with Pro-Mark "Signature" model drumsticks.

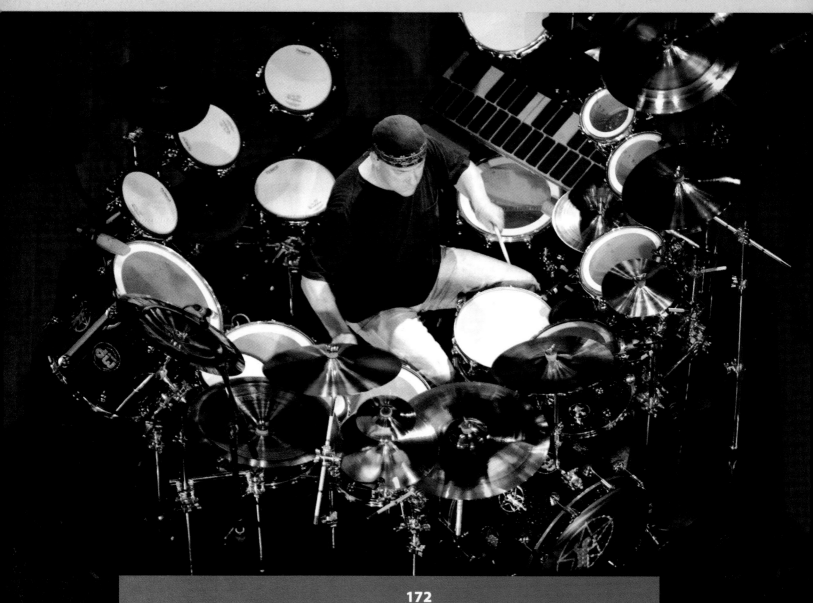

DRUM SETUP

Drums:

Drum Workshop Collector's Series (maple shells) in custom Black Mirra finish with Rush designs and logos

1. 16x22 bass drum
2. 6.5x14 snare drum (Solid Shell or Edge)
3. 7x8 tom
4. 7x10 tom
5. 8x12 tom
6. 9x13 tom
7. 12x15 floor tom
8. 16x16 floor tom
9. 16x18 floor tom
10. 3.5x13 snare drum
11. 13x15 floor tom

Cymbals:

Sabian Paragon series

A. 13" Paragon Hi-Hats
B. 10" Paragon Splash
C. 20" Paragon Crash
D. 16" Paragon Crash
E. 10" Paragon Splash
F. 16" Paragon Crash
G. 22" Paragon Ride
H. 14" Paragon Hi-Hats
I. 8" Paragon Splash
J. 18" Paragon Crash
K. 20" Paragon Chinese
L. 19" Paragon Chinese

Percussion & Electronics:

aa. MalletKAT electronic percussion controller
bb. cowbells
cc. Roland V-Drum (mounted in DW shell)
dd. Roland V-Cymbal
ee. Roland V-Hi-Hat
ff. FatKAT pedals (trigger for electronics)
gg. Dauz pad

Additional Electronics:
Roland TD-20X V-Drum brains (2)
Roland XV-5080 samplers
Glyph hard drives

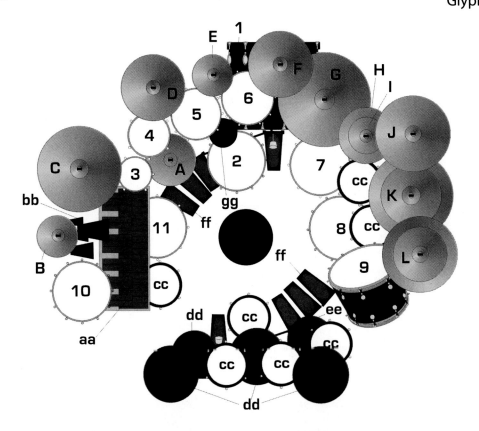

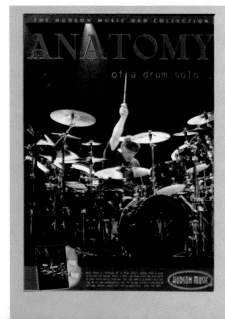

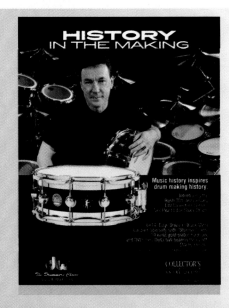

CHAPTER 14

The actual configuration for the drumset for the *Snakes & Arrows* tour wasn't much different from the previous few setups, since Neil had by now settled on a basic configuration that was comfortable for him. What differences there were—a strange size for the bass drum, advances in shell construction, new finish, and a new Chinese cymbal—are clearly detailed by Neil below.

As we have gone through the various eras of Rush's career and looked at all the different setups Neil has used, it is interesting to notice how his instrument has reflected the progression of the band's music. When you really think about it, it seems there are only a handful of highly influential drummers who have made changes as noticeable as Neil's during their careers (both in approach and setup). Buddy Rich, Charlie Watts, Ringo Starr, and countless others started with and stuck with a simple four-piece set (maybe with an extra floor tom here or there). Players like Simon Phillips and Steve Gadd have signature setups, but have not changed them very much throughout their careers. With Neil, on the other hand, you can almost tell what type of music Rush was making at any given time simply by looking at his setup. Bill Bruford and Terry Bozzio are two examples of drummers that do share this quality. Whether it's Neil's array of orchestral percussion instruments around him on the *Hemispheres* tour or the incorporation of Simmons drums for *Grace Under Pressure*, his instrument has reflected his playing in profound ways.

One thing that has allowed Neil to be much more "hands-on" with the design of his recent drumsets is the closeness of his relationship with DW. Living in Southern California, Neil is a short drive away from the factory. This gives him a place to rehearse for tours and practice for fun, and provides face time with the people who are building his instruments. This closeness with the company—along with their obvious passion for excellence—has inspired them to create unique, better-sounding, and totally customized instruments for him.

The *Snakes & Arrows* tour is represented in this book by two songs, "The Trees" and "Natural Science." These songs appear as bonus features on the *Taking Center Stage* DVD. "The Trees" is particularly interesting for showing how far electronic technology has come. The sounds of the V-Cymbals are quite convincing, and the ease of switching between sounds that Neil was so fascinated with in 1985 has become commonplace (check out the cool temple block and wind chime sounds in this song).

Neil used the *Snakes & Arrows* kit to record "BU2B" and "Caravan," since these two songs were recorded before the Time Machine tour and the rest of *Clockwork Angels* (2012).

From the Snakes & Arrows tour book, Neil writes:

After the 30th anniversary tour, the guys at Drum Workshop and I agreed that the R30 kit ought to be retired. I felt that way because it had been a true centerpiece of that tour (sitting center stage every night, after all), and I wanted to keep that "specialness." The DW guys, led by John Good ("the Wood Whisperer"), felt that way because they thought they could do better.

In 2006, they built me a "West Coast kit" on which I recorded a few songs for my friend Matt Scannell, as well as *Snakes & Arrows*. Everybody who heard those drums was blown away by their sound, but John continued to develop his ideas—combining different combinations of laminates for the shells, like his "Vertical Low Timbre" innovations. Just as the West Coast kit had eclipsed the R30 drums in tonality and resonance, these new ones take it to what my teacher, Freddie Gruber, would call "another place." After I had rehearsed for a couple of weeks on the West Coast kit, my drum tech, Lorne "Gump" Wheaton, put up the new ones, and I truly couldn't believe how different they sounded—how much bigger and warmer.

One of these drums actually is bigger—the 23" bass drum, which is another unique innovation of John Good's. Back in the '70s, when Rush were opening shows, I used to be able to go out front and listen to other drummers. I noticed then that 24" bass drums had a particular "kick" (for once that word is apt), but I preferred the playability and dynamics of a 22". John suspected that the 23" would combine the best of both, and he was right.

The "VLT" approach was also applied to the snare drum's shell, and it was another revelation—the best I have ever played, for both response and sound. The toms are 8", 10", 12", 13", two 15", 16", and 18", with DW's Coated Clear heads. Remo supplies some of the other heads, while the drumsticks are Pro-Mark "Signature" models.

In an earlier Web story, I hinted that "black is the new gold," and this time the hardware is plated in black nickel. Likewise, "red is the new black," the finish is Aztec Red, inset with a pair of logos Hugh Syme and I created for the CD package. The Greek symbol ouroboros, or snake eating its tail, surrounds a calligraphic rendering of my favorite road sign: the universal symbol for "winding road." (On a motorcycle or in a fast car, that's the best kind of "snake and arrow" you can see.) The repeating motif, in gold leaf and metallic gray satin over the Aztec Red, was created by DW's master painter, Louie Garcia (a true artist).

The cymbals are my signature Paragons, by Sabian, with a 22" ride, 20", 18", and two 16" crashes, 13" hi-hats, 14" "X-hats," 8" and 10" splashes, 19" and 20" China types, plus our new innovation, the "Diamondback," with tambourine jingles.

DW once again provided custom shells for the Roland V-Drums (the TD-20s), and the electronic stuff includes a MalletKAT, KAT trigger pedals, and a Dauz pad, all running through a Roland XV-5080 sampler and Glyph X-Project hard drives.

DRUM SETUP

Drums:

Drum Workshop Collector's Series (maple shells) in custom Aztec Red finish

1. 16x23 bass drum
2. 6.5x14 snare drum (straight VLT shell) (or 6.5x14 Edge)
3. 7x8 tom (VLT shell with 6-ply rings)
4. 7x10 tom (VLT shell with 6-ply rings)
5. 8x12 tom (VLT shell with 6-ply rings)
6. 9x13 tom (VLT shell with 3-ply rings)
7. 12x15 floor tom (VLT shell with 3-ply rings)
8. 16x16 floor tom
9. 16x18 floor tom
10. 3.5x13 snare drum (straight VLT shell)
11. 13x15 floor tom

Cymbals:

Sabian Paragon series

A. 13" Paragon Hi-Hats
B. 10" Paragon Splash
C. 20" Paragon Crash
D. 16" Paragon Crash
E. 10" Paragon Splash
F. 16" Paragon Crash
G. 22" Paragon Ride
H. 14" Paragon Hi-Hats
I. 8" Paragon Splash
J. 18" Paragon Crash
K. 20" Paragon Chinese
L. 20" Paragon Diamondback Chinese
M. 19" Paragon Chinese

Percussion & Electronics:

aa. MalletKAT electronic percussion controller
bb. cowbells
cc. Roland V-Drum (mounted in DW shell)
dd. Roland V-Cymbal
ee. Roland V-Hi-Hat
ff. FatKAT pedals (trigger for electronics)
gg. Dauz pad

Additional Electronics:
Roland TD-20X V-Drum brains (2)
Roland XV-5080 samplers
Glyph hard drives

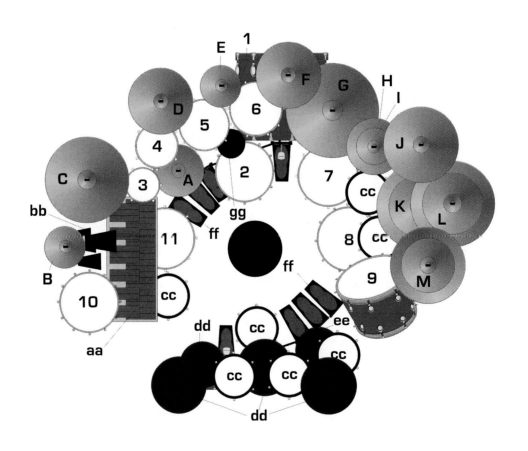

WORKIN' THEM ANGELS

Recorded for the *Snakes & Arrows* album (2007), "Workin' Them Angels" is interesting in the way it shifts between a 4/4 and 6/8 pulse. These shifts occur a few times throughout the song, with the eighth-note rate staying constant, and Neil uses some incredibly creative drum parts to smooth out the transitions.

To hear Neil give the 6/8 feel vastly different treatments, check out the second verse of "The Trees" and the guitar solo of "Free Will" in this book, and also give a listen to "Grand Finale" from *2112* and "Faithless" from *Snakes & Arrows*.

This song is one of three *Snakes & Arrows* tunes that were performed on the Time Machine tour (and appear on the *Taking Center Stage* DVD), the other two being "Far Cry" and "Faithless."

ANALYSIS:

"Workin' Them Angels" shifts between a "three" lilt and a straight "four" feel. Neil refers to the feeling of "three" on the DVD, and while the song could have been transcribed using 3/4 as a time signature, it is probably easier for drummers to understand the feel of these parts by seeing them written in 6/8, so that is what is used here. Note that when counting off the song, Neil plays all six eighth notes in the bar, and that is how the 6/8 sections should be felt at the top.

At measure 15, Neil introduces one of the main drumming themes of this song, an interesting "tribal" drum pattern using his deep toms. Pay close attention to the sticking here, which utilizes several right-hand strokes in a row to achieve the orchestration of pitches Neil wanted. What makes this part even more challenging is the fact that the feet are alternating underneath it in six.

After the tom part, at measure 19 the song breaks into 4/4, with Neil playing on the ride. As with many other songs in this book, you will see the unconventional way Neil plays with his left foot on the hi-hat while he plays the ride. In certain grooves, such as this one, he usually leaves out beat 1, plays beats 2 and 3, and then plays two eighth notes on beat 4 (beats "4 &"). This is something he probably arrived at naturally (as opposed to deliberately), and can be modified to something that feels easier for you if necessary. However, it is extremely interesting to hear the effect these left-foot patterns have on the feel of the groove.

Measures 34-38 contain an interesting and musically active transition from 4/4 back to 6/8, where Neil fills into the transition using the toms, then punctuates the band figures in 6/8, filling in between, and finally uses a long descending tom figure to settle back into the 6/8 lilt (which, at measure 39, takes on a more traditional feel of two groups of three notes per bar).

Other items of interest here include a fill transition in bars 76-77 that includes some flam accent-esque stickings followed by tom/double bass 32nd notes, and the reprise of the tribal tom theme, which is now juxtaposed dynamically with a quiet two measures of riding on the "Diamondback" Chinese cymbal (measures 88-93).

WORKIN' THEM ANGELS

WORKIN' THEM ANGELS

WORKIN' THEM ANGELS

slight rit - - - - -

FAR CRY

"Far Cry" is the opening track on *Snakes & Arrows* (2007), and it has all the hallmarks of a new Rush classic. The song contains all of the trademark Rush elements: energetic rock groove, great melody, interesting and musical use of odd time signatures, and all-around great playing with exciting parts from all three musicians.

This song received heavy analysis on the *Taking Center Stage* DVD because there are so many points of interest in the drum part. The PDF included on the DVD covered many of these parts, but here we get to take a look at the transcription of the song in its entirety. Neil has jam-packed this drum part with many of his signature concepts, yet in a seamless and musically appropriate way.

ANALYSIS:

"Far Cry" opens with a band unison figure that sounds fairly complex upon first listen, but breaks down to an easily understandable figure when you see it written out. This figure is a theme in the song, and appears three times. During the intro (measures 1-7), the drums play in unison with the guitar and bass, using snare and floor toms. When this theme reappears in measures 58-64, Neil embellishes the figure by adding crash cymbals and filling in the spaces between the accents with the ride cymbal. Finally, the theme reappears at the very end of the song (measures 95-103), where Neil solos over the figures. In this particular performance of the song, Neil stays very close to the solo that appears on the *Snakes & Arrows* album.

The intro groove (measures 8-17) also serves as the bridge of the song, and contains an interesting four-bar phrase that alternates between ending with a dropped beat (measures 11 and 16, which are in 3/4) and a straight bar of 4/4 (measures 15 and 17). The 4/4 endings contain a tasty double-bass/snare drum lick. Keep in mind when playing this groove that although it has some technical elements like the dropped beats, it still sounds like a big, fat rock groove, with loose hi-hats and heavy playing.

Measures 27-30 are the pre-chorus of the song (note that measures 27-28 repeat five times), with Neil playing a really fun, tasteful, and challenging groove. His right hand alternates between his ride cymbal and closed/mounted hi-hat (on the right), with a little bass-drum triplet lift into a China-cymbal accent at the end of every two bars. This is a great example of Neil's mastery of orchestration on the drumset. If you look over the drum parts in this book, you can see how his use of the China or splash cymbals is never haphazard, but chosen for the specific cymbal's appropriateness for the particular part of the song. You will notice that the left foot plays the hi-hat in this groove, and then moves over to the left bass-drum pedal to drop in a note of the triplet figure in the second bar. Although this seems difficult at first, the left-foot action in this groove actually ties the whole thing together nicely, and feels good to play once you are comfortable with it.

For the chorus of the song, appearing for the first time in bars 31-37, Neil plays his signature ride pattern. The last time Neil used this beat on a new song was on the *Roll the Bones* album in 1991, but at the request of producer Nick Raskulinecz, he brought it back here, and it fits perfectly. Note the left-foot hi-hat activity during this groove. In the chorus sections, in the first endings of the first two choruses (measures 36 and 55), Neil employs one of his signature fill devices: playing a quick set of four 32nd notes leading into 16ths. It is important to play these figures as all loud singles! This is how Neil articulates these types of fills so well when playing in large arenas and amphitheaters. Although Neil uses plenty of double strokes in other situations, these fast fills on the toms are always played with singles.

As the song builds to its climax, Neil becomes more active and exciting with the drum part, including an interesting syncopated fill in measure 86, and then a classic roundhouse two-bar fill in bars 91-92. Check out the crash-cymbal accent planted right in the middle of this fill! From a musical standpoint, notice that Neil chose to place this fill here, in an out-chorus section where the vocals have dropped out. One thing that many novice drummers don't notice is that Neil chooses to place these busy drum parts only in places where they don't step on the vocals. His musical choices are always careful.

Finally we come to the ending solo over the hits (bars 95-103). On the DVD Neil states that he aspires to get better at this type of soloing, and do more of it. The song "Mission" on *Hold Your Fire* (1987) is the only other Rush song with this type of short solo in it. Interestingly, that song was brought back for the *Snakes & Arrows* tour. Regarding the specific patterns Neil plays during the ending here, in measures 95-96 he states the band figures while filling softly in between them, then for the next three measures moves into some broken 16th and 32nd figures that refer to the ensemble figures. In bar 100 he rejoins the band to accent these rhythms together, and then for the final two bars, Neil plays in unison with the band on his large toms while filling in 16th-note triplet patterns with the feet. Danny Carey from Tool is a current master of this type of pattern, and uses it to great effect on many Tool songs.

FAR CRY

FAR CRY

FAR CRY

CHAPTER 15

CHAPTER 15

At last we come to Neil's current (as of 2012) drumset. The Time Machine kit far surpasses all of Neil's previous drumsets in terms of customization. The photos of the custom fittings on the copper-plated hardware give a clue as to the artistry, time, vision, and expense that went into creating this kit. The details are spelled out by Neil below, and for this tour, things are taken to an even higher level by the fact that the drum riser, amplifier coverings, and entire stage design all integrate the "steampunk" theme. This can best be described as a "retro-futuristic" motif, akin to how Jules Verne and his contemporaries imagined the future from their vantage point in the late 19th century.

The *Taking Center Stage* DVD documents this drumset visually and acoustically in a unique way, given the custom audio mix on the DVD. This mix not only brings the drums to the front, but thanks to engineer Sean McClintock, the drums were recorded to sound as close as possible to how the drums naturally sound. Neil paid a wonderful compliment to Sean on his success in achieving this by saying, "It sounds like me, playing my drums." The cymbals are also heard in a crystal-clear way, such that the minute details of how Neil attacks the hi-hat, or which section of the ride cymbal he chooses to play on, are made clearer than ever before.

Neil used this drumset to record the *Clockwork Angels* album (except for "BU2B" and "Caravan," which were recorded with the *Snakes & Arrows* kit), and on the *Clockwork Angels* tour for 2012 as well.

What will Neil's next crazy concept for a drumset be? We'll just have to wait and see. But one thing is sure: It will certainly be unique, creative, and state-of-the-art, just like the man himself.

From the Time Machine tour book, Neil writes:

Obviously the real time machine around here is the drumset.

And what a set of drums. Captain Nemo would have loved them, probably better than that dreary old pipe organ.

Drum Workshop really outdid themselves this time, spearheaded by Don Lombardi, John Good, Shon Smith, Garrison (like Madonna and Cher, he "dares to be known by one name alone"), hardware specialist Rich Sikra, and master painter Louis Garcia.

Barrel-stave redwood, copper leaf and silver alchemy symbols, and the innovation of copper hardware create the main visual statement, but the small, unique details of stand fittings and the little sculpted gears behind the lugs demonstrate DW's imaginative willingness to consider every possibility—and make it real.

Sonically, drum tech Lorne "Gump" Wheaton and I agree that these drums surpass all previous kits, in the richness of their tonality, and in the perfect blend of the individual drums with each other.

The custom stand fittings, drum hardware, and riser panels were designed by Greg Russell and Brian Walters of Tandem Digital. Their elaborate CG renderings of the kit and hardware helped to visualize the final outcome.

For their part, the Sabian cymbal company also got onboard with my wild ideas right away. Chris Stankee and Mark Love directed the development of a special steampunk design on the new "Brilliant" Paragons I've been using. (It took some experimenting with inks to find one that didn't affect the sound.)

Among other noisemakers, Gump and I include Pro-Mark sticks, DW and Remo heads, Roland V-Drums (with custom DW shells) (thanks Darren Shoepp), MalletKAT, KAT trigger pedals, and a Dauz pad, all running through a Roland XV-5080 sampler and Glyph X-Project hard drives.

DRUM SETUP

Drums:

Drum Workshop Collector's Series (maple shells) in custom Barrel-Stave Redwood finish

1. 16x23 bass drum (X-shell with 3-ply rings)
2. 6.5x14 snare drum (straight VLT shell) (or 6.5x14 Edge)
3. 7x8 tom (VLT shell with 6-ply rings)
4. 7x10 tom (VLT shell with 6-ply rings)
5. 8x12 tom (VLT shell with 6-ply rings)
6. 9x13 tom (VLT shell with 3-ply rings)
7. 12x15 floor tom (VLT shell with 3-ply rings)
8. 16x16 floor tom (X-shell with 3-ply rings)
9. 16x18 floor tom (X-shell with 3-ply rings)
10. 3.5x13 snare drum (straight VLT shell)
11. 13x15 floor tom (X-shell with 3-ply rings)

Cymbals:

Sabian Paragon series (except auxiliary hi-hats) in Brilliant finish with custom steampunk design

A. 13" Paragon Hi-Hats
B. 10" Paragon Splash
C. 20" Paragon Crash
D. 16" Paragon Crash
E. 10" Paragon Splash
F. 16" Paragon Crash
G. 22" Paragon Ride
H. 14" Vault Artisan Hi-Hats
I. 8" Paragon Splash
J. 18" Paragon Crash
K. 20" Paragon Chinese
L. 20" Paragon Diamondback Chinese
M. 19" Paragon Chinese

Percussion & Electronics:

aa. MalletKAT electronic percussion controller
bb. cowbells
cc. Roland V-Drum (mounted in DW shell)
dd. Roland V-Cymbal
ee. Roland V-Hi-Hat
ff. FatKAT pedals (trigger for electronics)
gg. Dauz pad

Additional Electronics:
Roland TD-20X V-Drum brains (2)
Roland XV-5080 samplers
Glyph hard drives

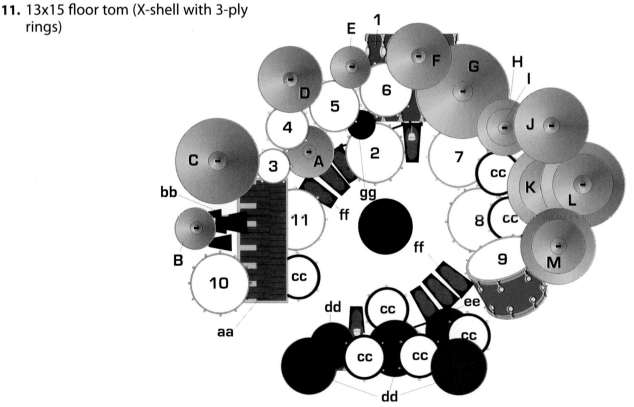

"BU2B" was released in 2010 as a two-song single (along with "Caravan") to kick off the Time Machine tour, and then appeared in the setlist on the tour. The song is a high-energy rocker with a heavy intro/verse section that verges on metal. The feel switches between a heavy half-time groove (with snare-drum backbeat on 3) and a double-time chorus (with snare drum on 2 and 4). Although they are known for using odd time signatures, Rush also plays high-energy rock tunes in straight 4/4, and this is one of them.

It is interesting that Neil's playing has definitely not mellowed on the last couple of albums. If anything, the band seems comfortable writing heavier material and Neil enjoys playing it loud and hard.

ANALYSIS:

During the intro of the song and several of the later sections, Neil rides on a crash cymbal, channeling an influence from Keith Moon. On the *Taking Center Stage* DVD, Neil mentions that he probably hasn't done this since the *2112* album in 1976, but here it fits the mood of the song perfectly. Notice that the intro and verse (measures 1-24) are in half-time as compared to the choruses that follow them.

At measure 17 Neil employs a signature device of his: an eighth/sixteenth-note ostinato between the ride and China cymbal, under which he constructs a half-time backbeat groove. You can hear him using a similar riding pattern on songs such as "New World Man," "The Enemy Within," and "The Manhattan Project" (using a splash instead of a China), among others. Take a look at the eight-bar phrase from measures 17-24 and notice how Neil keeps the cymbal ostinato going while he moves the snare and bass drum around to accent with the band. At the end of every second bar, there is also a crash cymbal that accents the "&" of 4. This crash breaks the ride/China flow. Watch the DVD to see how Neil executes this.

At measure 25, Neil makes the interesting choice of laying out for the first chorus. When he re-enters, playing on the hi-hat, the groove is at a double-time rate. Notice the energy shift that takes place because of this. Choosing when to employ a half-time or double-time feel change is an extremely useful tool for drummers to understand when constructing a drum part, because it is often a tool that can deliver a feel shift that is desired by the rest of the band, songwriter, or producer (depending on the situation).

This song features a few driving rock fills that match the energy of the track. Look at the fills in measures 100, 110, 114 to check out a device used by many classic rock drummers of Neil's era: playing eighth notes on the bass drum during a driving rock fill. If you watch the *Taking Center Stage* DVD carefully, you will see and hear how often Neil does this, and how often he actually plays soft, almost ghosted notes on the bass drum. During the 1960s and '70s, before bass drums were triggered and massive-sounding, drummers tended to be a little more free in using the bass drum in an active way underneath grooves, fills, and solos. Drummers like Keith Moon, Carmine Appice, and Bill Ward can be heard playing in this manner, and Neil comes from this rock tradition.

The fills in measures 126, 134-5, and 151 display Neil's always tasteful use of double bass. Although he has played a few grooves in recent years with steady double pedal ("One Little Victory," "Test for Echo"), he usually employs broken foot figures in grooves and fills, and this seems to fit well with Rush's music. If the nine-note grouping in measure 151 is confusing, just think of the hands playing quarter-note triplets, and fill in the alternating bass-drum strokes between the hand strokes.

BU2B

BU2B

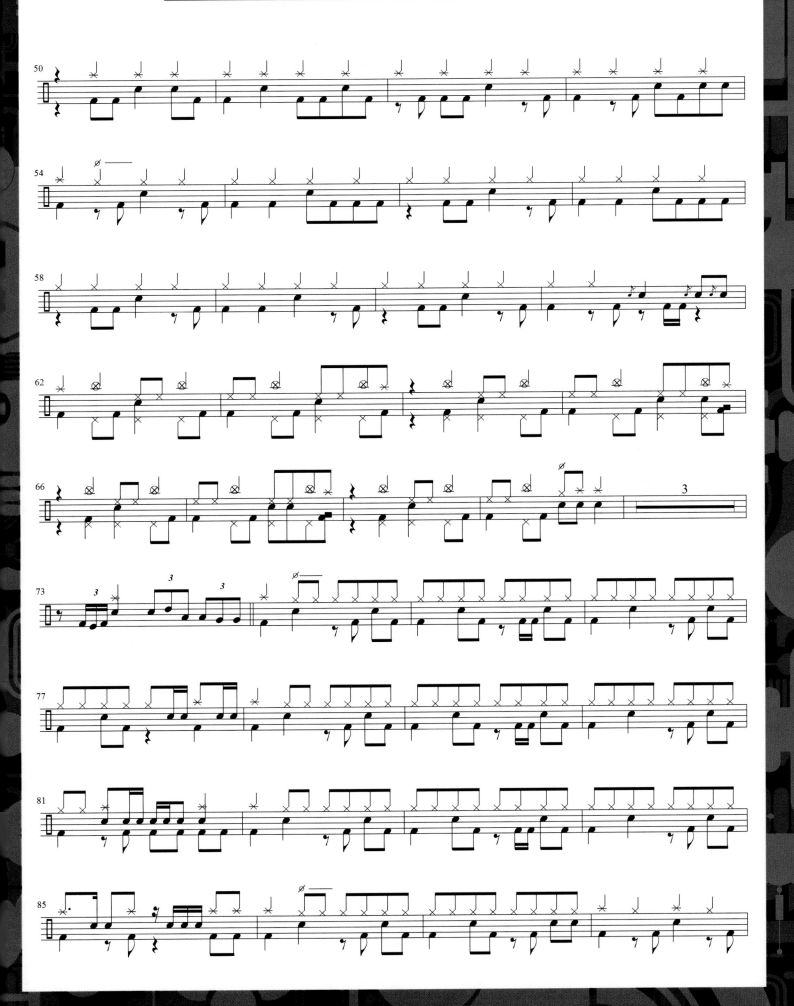

BU2B

BU2B

CARAVAN

"Caravan" is the second new song (along with "BU2B") to appear in the Time Machine set. Both of these songs appear on the 2012 album *Clockwork Angels.* "Caravan" is similar to "Far Cry" in that it incorporates odd time signatures and dropped beats into a heavy, grooving rock format. There is no sampling or triggering on the drums in the song; all the sounds are acoustic. Neil uses the entire kit, with his trademark creative and tasteful orchestrations.

On the *Taking Center Stage* DVD, "Caravan" is discussed in great detail in a featurette on disc 3, so please refer to that segment for further information about the song.

ANALYSIS:

The song begins with a brooding intro that Neil punctuates with his largest toms, and then launches into a driving rock groove. The fill in measure 24, like many other fills in the song, contains flam figures on the snare drum. Check out how cleanly they are executed. After the first verse, there are some ensemble figures connected by snare-drum rhythms (measures 34-35), and then a section (measures 36-44) that contains added beats. These added beats convert certain measures in the phrase to 6/4, and a kind of 3-against-2 feel is used between the bass drum and hi-hat (look at the last two beats of measure 37 for example, but notice that the rhythm is actually eighth and sixteenth notes). The end of this phrase, measure 44, contains four beats of this motif (two times through the figure), and then an added beat of rest which creates a "breath" before dropping into the chorus.

A half-time feel on the ride cymbal is played during the chorus, and once again we see some interesting left-foot hi-hat work to accompany it. Check out the use of the crash cymbals in measures 48 and 52. In subsequent choruses, Neil builds upon these ideas and makes them more complex as the song progresses. He does the same thing with some of the fills in the song. For instance, take a look at measures 73-74, and notice how these snare-drum figures are extended variations on what was played in measure 24. The next pre-chorus section (measures 75-83) follows the same form as the previous time, with the extended/added beats.

"Caravan" contains a challenging bridge/solo section which begins at measure 100, and contains lots of cool syncopations between the bass and drums (these are reflected by funky hi-hat and snare-drum patterns), and some very challenging fills. Measure 103 contains one of these syncopated fills, and measure 105 is a cool little rhythmic variation that incorporates the splash cymbal with some double bass. Following this section, starting at measure 111 there is an energetic "tribal war drums" section that uses a single-stroke sticking orchestrated among the low toms, with alternating eighth notes between the feet underneath. This leads up to the climactic fill in measures 118-119, which descends down the toms using flam figures, and then back up using fast singles.

Before the last chorus of the song, there is an interesting section beginning at measure 128 where Neil alternates his right hand between the ride cymbal and remote hi-hat, allowing him to drop some tasty double bass into the groove underneath. He punctuates this with some fills that also incorporate the double bass, like in measure 130. Note that this form basically follows the pre-chorus section, with the added beats creating measures of 6/4 time.

After the 5/4 bar at 141 (notice how Neil handles this measure differently each of the three times it occurs), the song drops into the last chorus. As it comes to a climax, Neil embellishes all of the different figures in the chorus, introducing triplets at measure 145, interesting snare and bass-drum interplay at measure 149, and one of his favorite hand-to-hand figures at measure 153. An intense double-bass fill in measure 157 leads to the last section of the tune, in which Neil channels Keith Moon. The quarter notes on the snare drum in measures 158-160, and the fill in measure 161 sound very much like The Who's drummer could be playing them. The song then returns briefly to a variation on its opening theme before the dynamic ending, which is comprised of a simple snare-drum crescendo.

CARAVAN

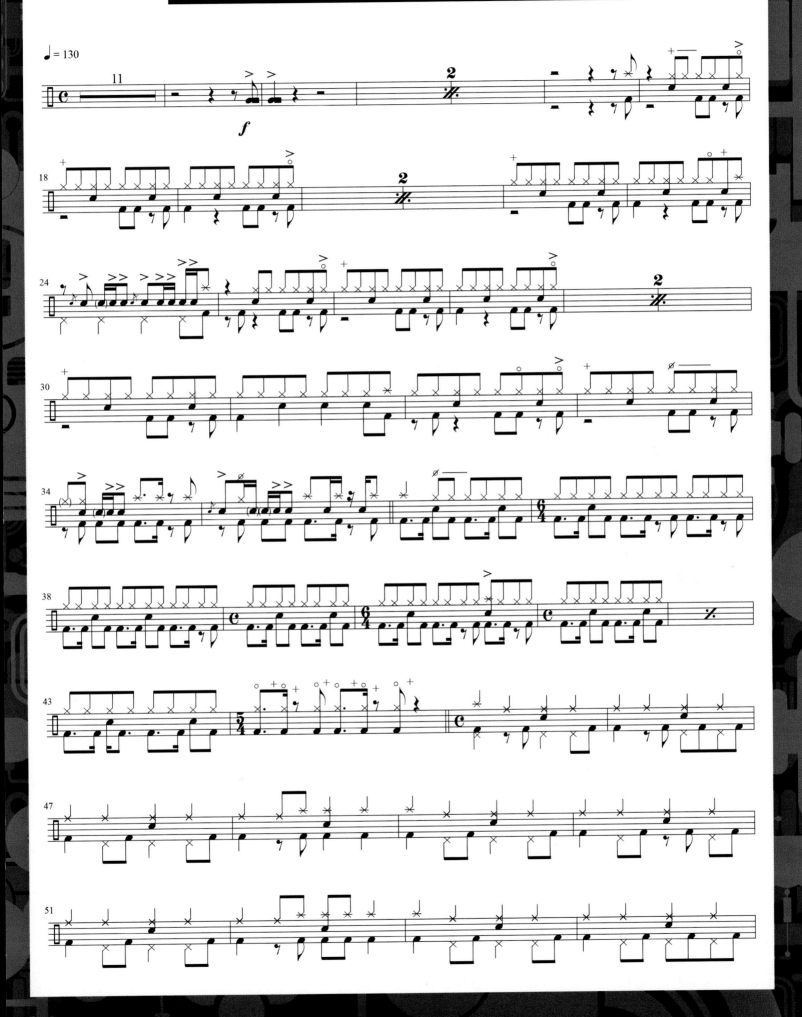

CARAVAN

CARAVAN

CARAVAN

SOURCE LIST

Books:

Rush: Merely Players by Robert Telleria, 2002, Quarry Press

Rush: Visions: The Official Biography by Bill Banasiewicz, 1988, Omnibus Press

Rush Official Tour Books 1976-2011:
A Farewell to Kings Tour Book, 1977
Hemispheres Tour Book, 1978
Permanent Waves Tour Book, 1980
Moving Pictures Tour Book, 1981
Signals/New World Tour Book, 1982
Grace Under Pressure Tour Book, 1984
Power Windows Tour Book, 1986
Hold Your Fire Tour Book, 1987
Presto Tour Book, 1990
Roll the Bones Tour Book, 1991
Counterparts Tour Book, 1994
Test for Echo Tour Book, 1996
Vapor Trails Tour Book, 2002
R30 Tour Book, 2004
Snakes & Arrows Tour Book, 2007
Time Machine Tour Book, 2011

All tour books © Anthem Entertainment. Neil Peart's writings used by permission of Anthem Entertainment and Mr. Peart.

Magazines:

Modern Drummer Magazine:
April-May 1980
April 1984
December 1989
February 1994
February 1995
September 2002
April 2006
August 2007
December 2011

Drum! Magazine:
October 2005
June 2007

Drumhead Magazine:
September-October 2007

DVDs/Blu-Ray:

Neil Peart: Taking Center Stage: A Lifetime of Live Performance, © 2011 Hudson Music
Rush: Time Machine Live in Cleveland, © 2011 Anthem Entertainment
Rush: Snakes & Arrows Tour, © 2008 Anthem Entertainment
Rush: Replay X3, © 2006 Anthem Entertainment/The Island Def Jam Music Group
Neil Peart: Anatomy of a Drum Solo, © 2005 Hudson Music
Rush: R30 Tour, © 2005 Anthem Entertainment
Rush in Rio, © 2003 Coming Home Studios/Anthem Entertainment
Rush: Chronicles, © 2001 Anthem Entertainment/The Island Def Jam Music Group
Neil Peart: A Work in Progress, © 1997 Alfred Music Publishing Co.

Websites:
www.rush.com
www.neilpeart.net
www.cygnus-x1.net
www.2112.net

SONGS

THE TREES
Words by NEIL PEART
Music by GEDDY LEE and ALEX LIFESON
© 1978 CORE MUSIC PUBLISHING
Used by Permission of ALFRED MUSIC PUBLISHING CO., INC.
All Rights Reserved

LA VILLA STRANGIATO
Words by NEIL PEART
Music by GEDDY LEE and ALEX LIFESON
© 1978 CORE MUSIC PUBLISHING
Used by Permission of ALFRED MUSIC PUBLISHING CO., INC.
All Rights Reserved

THE SPIRIT OF RADIO
Words by NEIL PEART
Music by GEDDY LEE and ALEX LIFESON
© 1980 CORE MUSIC PUBLISHING
Used by Permission of ALFRED MUSIC PUBLISHING CO., INC.
All Rights Reserved

FREE WILL
Words by NEIL PEART
Music by GEDDY LEE and ALEX LIFESON
© 1980 CORE MUSIC PUBLISHING
Used by Permission of ALFRED MUSIC PUBLISHING CO., INC.
All Rights Reserved

NATURAL SCIENCE
Words by NEIL PEART
Music by GEDDY LEE and ALEX LIFESON
© 1980 CORE MUSIC PUBLISHING
Used by Permission of ALFRED MUSIC PUBLISHING CO., INC.
All Rights Reserved

TOM SAWYER
Words by PYE DUBOIS and NEIL PEART
Music by GEDDY LEE and ALEX LIFESON
© 1981 CORE MUSIC PUBLISHING
Used by Permission of ALFRED MUSIC PUBLISHING CO., INC.
All Rights Reserved

YYZ
Music by GEDDY LEE and ALEX LIFESON
© 1981 CORE MUSIC PUBLISHING
Used by Permission of ALFRED MUSIC PUBLISHING CO., INC.
All Rights Reserved

SUBDIVISIONS
Words by NEIL PEART
Music by GEDDY LEE and ALEX LIFESON
© 1982 CORE MUSIC PUBLISHING
Used by Permission of ALFRED MUSIC PUBLISHING CO., INC.
All Rights Reserved

MARATHON
Words by NEIL PEART
Music by GEDDY LEE and ALEX LIFESON
© 1985 CORE MUSIC PUBLISHING
Used by Permission of ALFRED MUSIC PUBLISHING CO., INC.
All Rights Reserved

TIME STAND STILL
Words by NEIL PEART
Music by GEDDY LEE and ALEX LIFESON
© 1987 CORE MUSIC PUBLISHING
Used by Permission of ALFRED MUSIC PUBLISHING CO., INC.
All Rights Reserved

PRESTO
Words by NEIL PEART
Music by GEDDY LEE and ALEX LIFESON
© 1989, 1990 CORE MUSIC PUBLISHING
Used by Permission of ALFRED MUSIC PUBLISHING CO., INC.
All Rights Reserved

BRAVADO
Words by NEIL PEART
Music by GEDDY LEE and ALEX LIFESON
© 1991 CORE MUSIC PUBLISHING
Used by Permission of ALFRED MUSIC PUBLISHING CO., INC.
All Rights Reserved

LEAVE THAT THING ALONE!
Music by NEIL PEART, GEDDY LEE and ALEX LIFESON
© 1993 CORE MUSIC PUBLISHING
Used by Permission of ALFRED MUSIC PUBLISHING CO., INC.
All Rights Reserved

WORKIN' THEM ANGELS
Words by NEIL PEART
Music by GEDDY LEE and ALEX LIFESON
© 2007 CORE MUSIC PUBLISHING
Used by Permission of ALFRED MUSIC PUBLISHING CO., INC.
All Rights Reserved

FAR CRY
Words by NEIL PEART
Music by GEDDY LEE and ALEX LIFESON
© 2007 CORE MUSIC PUBLISHING
Used by Permission of ALFRED MUSIC PUBLISHING CO., INC.
All Rights Reserved

BU2B
Words and Music by NEIL PEART, GEDDY LEE and ALEX LIFESON
© 2010 CORE MUSIC PUBLISHING
Used by Permission of ALFRED MUSIC PUBLISHING CO., INC.
All Rights Reserved

CARAVAN
Words and Music by NEIL PEART, GEDDY LEE and ALEX LIFESON
© 2010 CORE MUSIC PUBLISHING
Used by Permission of ALFRED MUSIC PUBLISHING CO., INC.
All Rights Reserved

ABOUT THE AUTHOR

Joe Bergamini is a lifelong Rush fan who has maintained a diverse career as a drumming performer and educator for over 20 years. Though he enjoys various styles of playing, he is best-known for his progressive rock drumming

in the bands Happy the Man and 4Front. Joe is a fixture on the New York scene, and has performed in the Broadway productions of *Movin' Out*, *Jesus Christ Superstar* (2012 revival), *Rock of Ages*, *Jersey Boys*, *In the Heights*, *Million Dollar Quartet*, and *The Lion King*. He has also appeared on the first national tours of *Movin' Out* and *Jersey Boys*. For 11 years Joe was the drummer in the popular New York City-area Rush tribute band Power Windows, and has performed and recorded with many other artists as a sideman.

Recognized internationally as an educator, Joe has given hundreds of drum clinics at schools, retail stores, and conventions over the past 15 years. He has appeared at the Ultimate Drummers Weekend (Melbourne, Australia), the Cape Breton Drum Festival (Nova Scotia, Canada), KOSA (Vermont, USA), and the Sonny Emory Drum Camp (Atlanta, USA). In 2007 he was the featured drum clinician on the first Tama Dayz US tour. He also maintains a busy private teaching schedule at his studio in New Jersey. Among his many students who have gone on to pro careers is world-renowned jazz drummer Mark Guiliana.

Joe is very active in the music publishing world. He is the Senior Drum Editor for Hudson Music, where he oversees all book projects and acts as an associate producer on various DVD productions. In this capacity he has worked closely with some the world's greatest drummers in development of their educational products, including Neil Peart, Steve Smith, Stanton Moore, Gavin Harrison, John Blackwell, Aaron Spears, Keith Carlock, and many others.

The author of nine instructional drum books, Joe has won three *Modern Drummer* Readers Poll awards for his work. He was formerly Percussion Editor for Carl Fischer Publications, has worked on various promotional and R&D projects for Tama drums, is co-owner (with Dom Famularo) of Wizdom Media (an independent music publisher), and is an occasional writer for *Modern Drummer* magazine.

To find out more about Joe, and to check out his recordings and books, please visit his website at www.joebergamini.com.

Joe lives with his wife Kimberly and their two children in Whippany, New Jersey, USA.

NEIL PEART **dw** drums ENOUGH SAID.